Gluten-free Cooking

Sue Shepherd

Gluten-free Cooking

Sue Shepherd

Photography by Ian Wallace

PENGUIN

VIKING

VIKING

Published by the Penguin Group
Penguin Group (Australia)
250 Camberwell Road, Camberwell, Victoria 3124, Australia
(a division of Pearson Australia Group Pty Ltd)
Penguin Group (USA) Inc.
375 Hudson Street, New York, New York 10014, USA
Penguin Group (Canada)
90 Eglinton Avenue East, Suite 700, Toronto, Canada ON M4P 2Y3
(a division of Pearson Penguin Canada Inc.)
Penguin Books Ltd
80 Strand, London WC2R 0RL England
Penguin Ireland
25 St Stephen's Green, Dublin 2, Ireland
(a division of Penguin Books Ltd)
Penguin Books India Pvt Ltd
11 Community Centre, Panchsheel Park, New Delhi – 110 017, India
Penguin Group (NZ)
67 Apollo Drive, Rosedale, North Shore 0632, New Zealand
(a division of Pearson New Zealand Ltd)
Penguin Books (South Africa) (Pty) Ltd
24 Sturdee Avenue, Rosebank, Johannesburg 2196, South Africa

Penguin Books Ltd, Registered Offices: 80 Strand, London, WC2R 0RL, England

First published by Penguin Group (Australia), 2007

10 9 8 7 6 5 4

Text copyright © Sue Shepherd 2007
Photographs copyright © Ian Wallace 2007

The moral right of the author has been asserted

Design by Megan Baker © Penguin Group (Australia)
Cover and internal photography by Ian Wallace
Styling by Louise Pickford
Typeset in Frutiger by Post Pre-press Group, Brisbane, Queensland
Colour reproduction by Splitting Image, Clayton, Victoria
Printed and bound in Singapore by Imago Productions

National Library of Australia
Cataloguing-in-Publication data:

Shepherd, Sue.
   Gluten-free cooking

   Includes index.
   ISBN 978 0 670 07113 5.

   1. Malabsorption syndromes - Diet therapy - Recipes.
   2. Gluten-free diet - Recipes. 3. Milk-free diet - Recipes.
   4. Wheat-free diet - Recipes. 5. Celiac disease - Diet
   therapy - Recipes. 6. Irritable colon - Diet therapy -
   Recipes. I. Title.

641.5631

penguin.com.au

This book is dedicated to my dear,
enthusiastically supportive family

Contents

Introduction

This is a book for people who suffer from dietary problems, but who also love their food. My own experience and interests have taught me that the two are not in any way mutually exclusive.

In a strange twist of fate I was diagnosed as having coeliac disease while I was studying to become a dietitian. The news certainly changed my life, but I would definitely say for the better. Being a dietitian suits me down to the ground. Learning about digestion and the role of nutrients in the human body is a source of endless fascination for me; add to that my avid interest in food and my career path was clear. I specialise in the area of food intolerances, and gain so much pleasure from promoting all the great tastes that can still be enjoyed even if some foods are off your personal menu.

Over the years, it has become really important to me to make the most of my role as a dietitian and to promote awareness of food intolerances to the medical and general community. My PhD research investigated many aspects of health in relation to a gluten-free diet and dietary management of irritable bowel syndrome. My work has led to invitations to present at medical conferences around Australia and the world, and also to assist food companies in the development of new products.

Food is my passion. When I was first diagnosed with coeliac disease, the first thing I was given was a long list of foods I couldn't eat. As you can imagine, this was more than a little distressing – my daily food choices from that point on seemed so limited.

So I decided then and there to take a more positive approach when educating people about their special dietary needs; I was going to focus more on what they *could* enjoy rather than what they couldn't.

To this end I have started running supermarket tours to show people how to find safe, great-tasting foods; I have had a ball presenting at cooking demonstrations and working on morning television; I have organised gluten-free/wheat-free food expos and have been gratified to achieve attendances of over 10,000 people; and I have written cookbooks – all to promote fabulous flavours that just happen to be gluten- and wheat-free.

As a little girl I was encouraged to experiment in the kitchen (potato-skin soup anyone?) so I have always felt comfortable playing with different flavours and trying out new recipes. I am so proud to present my latest gluten-free cookbook. Many people suffering from coeliac disease, fructose malabsorption, lactose intolerance or irritable bowel syndrome do not consider food their friend. Well I beg to differ. I believe that every recipe in this book will enable you to really enjoy your food and feel well.

Best wishes for good health,

Sue Shepherd

Food Intolerances

Coeliac disease

Coeliac disease is a medically diagnosed condition of an intolerance to gluten in the diet. Gluten is the protein component of wheat, rye, barley and oats. In people with coeliac disease, gluten causes damage to the lining of the small intestine (villi). As a result, the ability to absorb nutrients is dramatically decreased and people can become very unwell. Typical symptoms can include bloating, wind, pain, diarrhoea or constipation or a combination of both, fatigue and iron deficiency.

Coeliac disease is a life-long condition treated by a diet free from all gluten. This prevents further damage to the villi and allows them to return to normal, so that nutrients can be properly absorbed.

The gluten-free diet permits fruits, vegetables, unprocessed meat, fish and chicken, eggs, nuts, seeds, legumes and lentils, most dairy foods, oils and margarines.

Breads, pasta and cereals can be made from alternative sources, such as corn, rice, soy, potato and tapioca. There are also many specialty gluten-free products available.

For most people diagnosed as requiring a gluten-free diet, the change in lifestyle can seem overwhelming. Learning which foods are suitable and which foods are no longer permitted is time-consuming at first, and the diet can seem very restrictive. *Gluten-free Cooking* shows you how to fully enjoy the great tastes of a gluten-free diet and is suitable for people with coeliac disease and the related skin condition of dermatitis herpetiformis.

While every effort has been made to indicate gluten-free ingredients in this book, it is essential to read the ingredients list of all food products to determine if they are suitable for inclusion in the gluten-free diet. The recipes in this book comply with the Australian gluten-free food standard at the time of printing.

Lactose intolerance

Lactose intolerance can be a cause of symptoms of irritable bowel syndrome. These include bloating, wind, pain, nausea, diarrhoea and/or constipation. Additionally, many people with coeliac disease can have a secondary lactose intolerance. In such people, the lactose intolerance is usually only temporary, caused by gluten-induced damage in the small intestine. In some, however, it is a condition that will remain for life.

Lactose is a naturally occurring sugar that is found in cow's, goat's and sheep's milk. Typically, in people with lactose intolerance, the body stops making enough of the enzyme lactase, which breaks down the sugar lactose. However, people can differ in the severity of their intolerance. Most people are able to tolerate small amounts of lactose in their diet.

Lactose is present in large amounts in milk, ice cream and custard. It is present in moderate amounts in yoghurt and soft/unripened cheeses (for example, cottage, ricotta, quark, cream cheeses). Cream contains a minimal amount of lactose. Hard/ripened cheeses (cheddar, parmesan, camembert, edam, gouda, blue vein, mozzarella, etc) and butter are virtually free of lactose.

The majority of recipes in *Gluten-free Cooking* are lactose-free or contain only minimal amounts of lactose. Recipes that are not suitable or require modification are marked ◇.

Fructose malabsorption

Fructose malabsorption is a condition where the small intestine is impaired in its ability to absorb fructose (a naturally occurring sugar). Fructose malabsorption is a different condition to hereditary fructose intolerance.

When fructose is not absorbed properly in the small intestine, it can travel through to the large intestine where bacterial fermentation can cause symptoms of irritable bowel syndrome.

Although fructose is present in one form or another in virtually every fruit, and in many vegetables and grains, it isn't all bad news. Not every food that contains fructose needs to be avoided by people with fructose malabsorption.

The most commonly consumed 'problem' foods are:

Fruits: apple, pear, mango, watermelon, quince, paw paw (papaya), lychee, guava and pomegranate. In excess, the following are also problematic: dried fruit, fruit juice and tomato paste.

Vegetables: onion, spring onion (scallion), leek, asparagus, artichoke, Jerusalem artichoke, witlof (Belgian endive), endive, chicory, radicchio and dandelion greens.

Others: honey, coconut cream and large quantities of wheat. Fructose, fruit juice sweeteners (apple juice concentrate, pear pastes) and high-fructose corn syrups are ingredients that have high levels of fructose and are a problem in large amounts.

You will note that some ingredients in the recipes are specified as 'gluten-free'. Gluten is in wheat, rye, barley and sometimes oats. People with fructose malabsorption find wheat, not gluten, is a problem food when consumed in large amounts, and so they can generally eat rye, barley and oats. It is not essential to follow a gluten-free diet if you have fructose malabsorption, however, as the recipes in this cookbook are gluten-free, they are all also wheat-free.

Even though the recipes are all formulated with ingredients that are suitable for fructose malabsorption, if you suffer from this condition, you should limit your serving size of any fruit-based dish to that which is indicated in the recipe. Consuming large quantities of even 'safe' fruits can cause symptoms.

If you have noticed you feel better on a wheat-free diet, you may have fructose malabsorption. However, coeliac disease may also be a possibility. You should discuss tests for coeliac disease with your doctor (see the section on irritable bowel syndrome below for more information). Some people can have both coeliac disease and fructose malabsorption.

Irritable bowel syndrome

Irritable bowel syndrome is a condition that affects approximately 15 per cent of the population. Symptoms include abdominal pain or discomfort associated with alteration of bowel habits (diarrhoea, constipation or a combination of both). Wind, bloating and a feeling of incomplete evacuation are also common symptoms. These symptoms fluctuate in their severity from day to day and week to week.

The diagnosis is made on the pattern of the symptoms. One condition that can mimic irritable bowel syndrome is coeliac disease. Simple screening blood tests are now readily available. Ask your doctor for blood tests to investigate for coeliac disease. You do need to be eating gluten in your diet for the tests to be useful. If the tests are positive, it does not necessarily mean you have coeliac disease, but you should have a small bowel biopsy to make the diagnosis. Talk to your doctor or gastroenterologist for more information.

There is no one diet that will suit every person who suffers from irritable bowel syndrome. The recipes developed for *Gluten-free Cooking* use foods that are low in FODMAPs™ – a group of poorly absorbed food molecules that can cause symptoms of irritable bowel syndrome in many people. FODMAP™ foods include wheat, high-fructose foods and also foods containing lactose, sorbitol (commonly found in stone fruits) and raffinose (commonly found in lentils, legumes, onion, cabbage and brussels sprouts). People with

irritable bowel syndrome often find that reducing the wheat and dairy in their diet is helpful in minimising symptoms. As all the recipes in *Gluten-free Cooking* are wheat-free, and most are lactose-, raffinose- and sorbitol-free, they will be suitable. The small number of recipes that do contain lactose, sorbitol or raffinose have notes to that effect.

High-fat foods often aggravate symptoms of irritable bowel syndrome so low-fat ingredients are encouraged. Most recipes in *Gluten-free Cooking* are not high in fat.

For more information see www.coeliac.com.au

Equipping Your Kitchen

As some of the following pantry items may require a trip to a specialty store, buy more than you need so you have a good supply on hand. See the glossary on page 137 for more information on unfamiliar ingredients.

Flours

Essential:

Cornflour (cornstarch) – must be made from maize (corn); available in supermarkets

Potato flour – available at Asian grocery stores

Rice flour – preferably fine rice flour; available at Asian grocery stores

Soy flour – available in health-food shops (look for debittered varieties)

Tapioca flour – available at Asian grocery stores

Worthwhile:

Amaranth flour – available in health-food shops

Arrowroot – available in supermarkets

Besan/chickpea flour – an alternative to soy, available in health-food shops and Indian grocery stores

Buckwheat flour – available in health-food shops (be aware some are blends and contain wheat flour)

Millet flour – available in health-food shops

Quinoa flour – pronounced 'keen-wah'; available in health-food shops

Others

Almond meal – available in supermarkets

Dried yeast – ensure it is gluten-free; available in supermarkets

Gluten-free baking powder – available in supermarkets

Gluten-free breadcrumbs – available in supermarkets

Gluten-free gravy – available in supermarkets

Pure icing (confectioner's) sugar – available in supermarkets

Soy sauce – ensure it is gluten-free; available in supermarkets

Stock cubes – ensure they are gluten-free; available in supermarkets

Xanthan gum – available in health-food shops

Baking Tips

- There is no one flour that substitutes directly for wheat flour. A combination of gluten-free flours (usually three or more) works best. A good all-purpose gluten-free flour blend is:
  - 2 parts (fine) rice flour
  - 1 part soy flour (debittered)
  - 1 part EITHER potato flour OR maize cornflour (cornstarch) OR tapioca flour

- Vegetable gums such as xanthan gum, guar gum and CMC (carboxymethyl cellulose) can be used in baking recipes to play the role of a 'gluten substitute' by helping to improve the elasticity and crumb structure in baked goods.

- Gluten-free flour blends should be sifted three times to ensure the flours are evenly mixed and aerated. Raising agents (for example, gluten-free baking powder and bicarbonate of soda) and vegetable gums should be sifted together with the flours.

- Gluten-free baked goods can tend to dry out more quickly than wheat-based versions so it is a good idea to cut cakes into slices, or bake the mixture in muffin tins, and freeze the excess portions. They will defrost well and this practice will help ensure they are fresh for a later day. Dry or stale gluten-free baked goods can be rejuvenated in the microwave for 20–30 seconds on high.

- Separate gluten-containing and gluten-free ingredients in the pantry to avoid the risk of accidentally choosing the wrong type. Label clearly if repackaging ingredients in your own containers.

- Use baking paper when baking. It's terrific for lining cake tins and biscuit trays, and it really makes life easier if you roll gluten-free pastry between two sheets.

- Gluten-free baking is often less forgiving than wheat-based so make sure you follow the recipe strictly. Ensure your oven temperature is accurate and follow the suggested cooking times to give the best results.

- A word of warning for those of you who like to lick the bowl: while it is important to use soy flour in gluten-free baking, the raw cookie dough or cake batter can taste a little bitter. Please don't be put off – the bitter taste disappears when cooked. You can buy debittered soy flour, and this is recommended.

Breakfasts

Get up and go – gluten-free! Breakfast really does help improve our concentration and performance.

Breakfast is a meal that can seem problematic when following a gluten-free diet, as so many of the usual breakfast options are wheat-based: cereals, toast, crumpets, muffins and pancakes. Even porridge is off menu for those on a gluten-free diet.

It is likely you have heard somewhere along the way that breakfast is the most important meal of the day. It really does help improve our concentration and performance (both for kids at school and big kids at work). It can also help satisfy our appetite so that we don't fall into the trap of snacking on less nutritious foods late morning because we haven't got off to a more nourishing start to the day.

So I have put together some suggestions for everyday gluten-free breakfast solutions, as well as a few recipes for special breakfasts, for when you have time to really sit and enjoy this delicious start to the day.

Gluten-free breakfast cereals Although cornflakes and rice puffs may seem an obvious choice, be aware that many contain malt as an ingredient (and are therefore not gluten-free), and in terms of nutrition they are usually fairly low in fibre. Explore the ever-increasing range of cereals that are now available and try to make a higher-fibre choice: look at specialty mueslis, or consider adding a handful of nuts, seeds or dried fruit to lower-fibre cereals.

Gluten-free toast There are so many varieties of gluten-free bread available these days – try them all to find one that works for you, then top with gluten-free spreads or pop a slice of cheese on top and place under the grill.

Everyday breakfast ideas

- Fresh fruit – whole, or cut up into pieces for a platter or fruit salad

- Tinned fruit, drained of syrup or juice

- Yoghurt – natural or gluten-free fruit yoghurt

- Smoothies (see page 65)

- Eggs – boiled, poached, scrambled or fried in a non-stick pan

- Baked beans (check they are gluten-free) on gluten-free toast

- A gluten-free fry up: bacon, spinach, tomatoes and eggs

Weekend Breakfasts

- **Spinach Eggs with Roasted Balsamic Tomatoes:**
  Preheat the oven to 180°C (350°F). Grease
  4 ramekin dishes. Cut 4 large roma (plum)
  tomatoes in half and place on a baking tray.
  Drizzle with 1 tablespoon olive oil and 1 tablespoon
  balsamic vinegar, and season to taste. Roast for
  20 minutes. Divide 2 cups baby spinach leaves
  evenly among the ramekin dishes and season well.
  Break an egg over the top of each, then gently tilt
  the ramekin to ensure the egg white runs through
  the spinach. Place the ramekins in a large frying pan
  with a lid. Pour boiling water into the pan to come
  halfway up the sides of the ramekin dishes, then
  cover and cook for 10–12 minutes or until done to
  your liking. Gently remove the spinach eggs from
  the ramekins. Serve with the roasted tomatoes on
  toasted gluten-free bread. *Serves 4*

- **Cheese and Mustard Hash Browns:** Grate 400 g
  (14 oz) pontiac potatoes, squeeze out any excess
  liquid then leave to drain in a metal sieve for about
  10 minutes. Place the grated potato, 1 beaten egg,
  1 tablespoon gluten-free cornflour (cornstarch),
  1 tablespoon wholegrain mustard and ½ cup
  grated parmesan in a medium bowl and season
  to taste with salt and freshly ground black pepper.
  Combine well, then shape the mixture into four
  small cakes about 5 cm (2 inches) in diameter. Heat
  a little olive oil in a medium frying pan over medium
  heat, add the hash browns and pan-fry for about
  2 minutes each side or until cooked through and
  golden brown. Delicious served warm with eggs,
  wilted spinach or roasted tomatoes. *Serves 2*

- **Cinnamon Banana Pancakes:** Sift ⅔ cup fine rice flour, 3 tablespoons soy flour, 4 tablespoons gluten-free cornflour (cornstarch), ¾ teaspoon bicarbonate of soda and ¼ teaspoon ground cinnamon three times into a large bowl. Combine 2 beaten eggs, 150 ml (5 fl oz) low-fat milk, 2 tablespoons brown sugar and 1 mashed banana in another bowl. Pour into the dry ingredients and stir well. Stir in 40 g (1½ oz) melted butter. Leave to sit for 10 minutes. Heat a medium frying pan over low–medium heat for 2 minutes. Spray with non-stick spray, then pour in 3–4 tablespoons of batter for each pancake. Cook for 2–3 minutes or until bubbles start to appear, then flip and cook for 2 minutes on the other side. Remove from the pan, cover and keep warm while you make the remaining pancakes. To serve, drizzle with golden or maple syrup and top with toasted slivered almonds. *Serves 4*

- **Smoked Salmon Scrambled Eggs:** Place 10 eggs, ½ cup milk, 4 tablespoons sour cream and some freshly ground black pepper in a large bowl and whisk together well. Melt 40 g (1½ oz) butter in a medium frying pan over low heat and pour in the egg mixture. Use a wooden spoon to gently push the mixture into the middle of the pan – do this every 10 seconds or so to prevent sticking. Cook for 5 minutes or until the egg is almost cooked – you still want the mixture to be creamy and slightly runny. Stir in 100 g (3½ oz) sliced smoked salmon just before serving. Sprinkle with 1 tablespoon finely chopped dill and serve with toasted gluten-free bread. *Serves 4*

◊ *The milk in the Cinnamon Banana Pancakes and Smoked Salmon Scrambled Eggs can be replaced with lactose-free milk.*

Soups and Light Meals

Sesame Chicken Salad

The preparation of the chicken for this salad is essential as it ensures the breast is nice and tender. There is nothing worse than dry chicken in a salad!

Serves 4

1 egg white, lightly beaten

½ teaspoon salt

1 tablespoon lemon juice

1 tablespoon gluten-free cornflour (cornstarch)

500 g (1 lb 2 oz) skinless chicken breast, sliced

2 tablespoons sesame oil

2 tablespoons sesame seeds

SALAD

100 g (3½ oz) baby spinach leaves

1 cup snow pea sprouts

200 g (7 oz) snow peas (mange-tout), topped
  and tailed, cut in half

200 g (7 oz) cherry tomatoes, halved

1 avocado, diced

½ green capsicum (pepper), seeded and
  cut into strips

DRESSING

1 tablespoon sesame oil

3 tablespoons sushi vinegar

1 clove garlic, crushed

1 tablespoon chopped coriander (cilantro)
  leaves

½ cup peanuts, roughly chopped

Combine the egg white, salt, lemon juice and cornflour in a bowl. Coat the chicken strips in the mixture, then cover and refrigerate for 30 minutes.

Meanwhile, mix the salad ingredients together in a large bowl. Put the dressing ingredients in a screw-top jar and shake well.

Fill a medium saucepan with water and bring to the boil. Add 1 tablespoon sesame oil. Place the chicken in the boiling water, stir quickly for 1 minute, then remove immediately and drain.

Heat the remaining sesame oil in a small frying pan over medium–high heat. Add the poached chicken pieces and sesame seeds, and cook for 3–5 minutes or until browned.

Pour the salad dressing over the salad and toss to combine well. Top with the chicken pieces and serve.

Lemon Herb Squid

The fresh flavours of lemon and herbs work so well with the squid. Served with a fresh green salad, this is the perfect light lunch.

Serves 4

4 large or 8 regular squid bodies (tubes), rinsed

3 tablespoons olive oil

2 tablespoons lemon juice

2 tablespoons finely grated lemon zest

½ cup chopped oregano

½ cup chopped parsley

½ teaspoon salt

freshly ground black pepper

GARDEN SALAD

150 g (5½ oz) lettuce leaves, roughly chopped

½ large cucumber, diced

1 avocado, sliced

2 stalks celery, thinly sliced

½ green capsicum (pepper), seeded and diced

1 cup snow pea sprouts

DRESSING

3 tablespoons olive oil

1½ tablespoons lemon juice

½ fresh red chilli, seeded and finely chopped

½ teaspoon brown sugar

salt

Cut the squid bodies down the long sides to make two large pieces (if using large squid, cut into quarters). With a sharp knife, cut the squid pieces in a 1 cm (½ inch) criss-cross pattern, cutting about three-quarters of the way through (don't cut all the way through). This ensures the squid will curl when cooked.

Combine the olive oil, lemon juice, lemon zest, oregano, parsley, salt and pepper in a large bowl. Add the squid pieces and toss to coat in the mixture. Cover and refrigerate for 3–4 hours.

To make the salad, combine the lettuce, cucumber, avocado, celery, capsicum and snow pea sprouts in a large bowl. Divide among four serving plates.

To make the dressing, put the olive oil, lemon juice, chilli, brown sugar and salt in a screw-top jar and shake well.

Place the squid pieces, scored-side down, on a preheated barbecue, chargrill pan or frying pan and cook over high heat for 2–3 minutes. Turn and cook for 1–2 minutes or until chargrilled in appearance.

Shake the dressing and drizzle over the salad. Arrange the squid on top and serve warm.

Chicken and Corn Soup

My cookbook would not be complete without this old favourite, enjoyed by so many.

Serves 4

4 cups gluten-free chicken stock
500 g (1 lb 2 oz) skinless chicken breast, cut into very thin slices
2 x 420 g (15 oz) tins gluten-free creamed corn
4 eggs, lightly beaten
salt
freshly ground black pepper

In a large heavy-based saucepan, bring the chicken stock to the boil. Add the chicken, reduce the heat and simmer for 5 minutes. Add the creamed corn and simmer for a further 5 minutes.

Stir the soup rapidly and drizzle in the beaten egg. Continue stirring to ensure the egg is separated and spread evenly through the soup. Season with salt and pepper before serving.

Thai Basil Salad

Mmmm basil, one of the great-tasting signature Thai herbs. This salad also works really well with chicken or beef instead of the tofu.

Serves 4

100 g (3½ oz) mung bean vermicelli (glass) noodles
2 red capsicums (peppers), seeded and cut into thin strips
1 cup bean sprouts
1 cucumber, halved and sliced
½ cup unsalted cashews, toasted
1½ cups basil, chopped
200 g (7 oz) puffed tofu squares, cut into 1 cm (½ inch) cubes
whole basil leaves, extra, to garnish

DRESSING
3 tablespoons lime juice
1½ tablespoons fish sauce
1½ tablespoons brown sugar
1 teaspoon sesame oil

Soak the noodles in a large bowl of hot water for about 4–5 minutes or until softened. Drain, rinse under cold water, drain again and set aside.

Place the noodles, capsicum, bean sprouts, cucumber, cashews and basil in a large bowl. Toss gently to combine.

To make the dressing, put the lime juice, fish sauce, brown sugar and sesame oil in a screw-top jar and shake well.

Add the tofu to the salad, drizzle on the dressing and toss to combine. Garnish with the extra basil leaves.

Thai Basil Salad

Crab and Chilli Omelette

This recipe shows how easily crab can be incorporated into an omelette base, and with the addition of chilli, this dish really sings.

Serves 4

8 eggs

200 g (7 oz) fresh crab meat

½ cup grated cheddar

1–2 small fresh red chillies, seeded and chopped

1 clove garlic, crushed

1 tablespoon chopped parsley

salt

freshly ground black pepper

1 tablespoon sesame oil

½ cup grated cheddar, extra

Preheat the oven to 150°C (300°F).

Whisk together the eggs, crab meat, cheddar, chilli, garlic, parsley, salt and pepper in a medium mixing bowl. Heat the sesame oil in a small frying pan over medium heat. Add a quarter of the mixture to the pan and cook until almost set on top. Carefully lift at the edges with a spatula, and shake the omelette loose. Place the pan under a hot grill to finish the cooking process.

Sprinkle a handful of the extra cheddar evenly over half the omelette, then fold over to encase the cheese. Keep warm in the oven while cooking the remaining omelettes. Alternatively, cook all the eggs together in a large frying pan and cut the omelette into quarters before serving.

Moroccan Soup

A deliciously hearty soup that really fills and warms the stomach. The Moroccan flavours complement the tender lamb shanks beautifully.

Serves 4–6

2 tablespoons olive oil

2 cloves garlic, crushed

1 teaspoon ground coriander

1½ teaspoons ground cumin

½ teaspoon turmeric

¼ teaspoon cayenne pepper

3 lamb shanks

1 kg (2 lb 4 oz) carrots, chopped

1 cup white rice

410 g (14½ oz) tin chopped tomatoes

12 cups gluten-free vegetable stock

salt

freshly ground black pepper

Place the olive oil, garlic and spices in a large stockpot over medium–high heat and cook, stirring, for 1–2 minutes to allow the flavours to develop. Add the lamb shanks, toss through the spice mix to coat and cook for 5–7 minutes or until lightly browned on all sides.

Stir in the carrot, rice, tomatoes and vegetable stock and bring to the boil. Reduce the heat to medium–low and simmer, stirring occasionally, for 1–1½ hours or until the meat is falling off the bone. Remove the shanks from the pan and shred the meat. Return the shredded meat to the soup and stir through. Season to taste and serve.

Garlic, Spinach and Potato Quiche

A rice-base crust can be used instead of pastry if preferred – just mix 3 cups of cooked white rice and one beaten egg and press into the flan tin.

Serves 8–10

PASTRY

130 g (4½ oz) fine rice flour

75 g (2½ oz) gluten-free cornflour (cornstarch)

45 g (1½ oz) soy flour

1 teaspoon xanthan gum (optional)

160 g (5¾ oz) cold butter

4–5 tablespoons iced water

FILLING

2 potatoes, cut into cubes

20 g (¾ oz) butter

3 cloves garlic, crushed

6 eggs

1 cup reduced-fat evaporated milk

250 g (9 oz) chopped cooked spinach

1 cup grated reduced-fat cheddar

salt

freshly ground black pepper

To make the pastry, combine the sifted flours, xanthan gum and butter in a food processor until it resembles fine breadcrumbs. Continue processing and add the iced water 1 tablespoon at a time until the mixture forms a soft dough. Less water will be required in a warm kitchen! Turn out the dough onto a board dusted with gluten-free cornflour and knead for 1–2 minutes. Wrap in plastic film and rest in the refrigerator for 30 minutes.

Preheat the oven to 170°C (325°F). Grease a 23 cm (9 inch) fluted flan tin.

Roll out the pastry between two sheets of non-stick baking paper until large enough to line the flan tin. Place gently in the tin and trim the edges. Line the pastry with baking paper and fill with baking beads or uncooked rice. Blind-bake for 10–15 minutes or until lightly browned. Remove from oven and reduce the temperature to 160°C (315°F).

To make the filling, cook the potato in a medium saucepan of boiling water for 3–4 minutes or until just tender. Drain. Heat the butter and garlic in a non-stick frying pan over medium heat. Add the potato and cook, stirring, for 3–4 minutes or until golden.

Whisk the eggs in a medium mixing bowl, then add the evaporated milk, spinach and cheddar; season to taste. Arrange the potato over the pastry base and pour the egg mixture over the top. Bake for 45 minutes or until cooked through and set when shaken gently.

◇ *This recipe is unsuitable for people with lactose intolerance unless consumed as a small serve.*

Cream of Vegetable Soup

There are so many recipes for vegetable soup. I'm sure you're going to love this version – the celeriac gives a great flavour base.

Serves 4–6

30 g (1 oz) butter

350 g (12 oz) celeriac, peeled, halved and cut into
    5 mm (¼ inch) thick slices

2 heads broccoli, cut into chunks (including stalks)

3 swedes (rutabagas), cut into chunks

2 large carrots, cut into chunks

400 g (14 oz) pumpkin, cut into chunks

3 potatoes, cut into chunks

4 cups gluten-free vegetable stock

1½ cups reduced-fat evaporated milk

salt

freshly ground black pepper

Place a large heavy-based stockpot over medium heat, melt the butter and sauté the celeriac until golden brown. Add the broccoli, swede, carrot, pumpkin and potato, then pour in the vegetable stock. Bring to the boil, then reduce the heat and simmer, covered, for 1 hour.

Remove the pot from the heat and leave to cool to room temperature. Use a hand-held blender to puree the vegetables to a smooth consistency (alternatively, place in a food processor and process until smooth). Stir in the evaporated milk, and season to taste with salt and pepper.

◇ *Evaporated milk can be replaced with lactose-free milk.*

Cauliflower and Cheese Soup

People who like big-flavoured soup will really enjoy this one. The combination of cheeses adds a depth of flavour that carries through every mouthful.

Serves 4

50 g (1¾ oz) butter

2 kg (4 lb 8 oz) cauliflower, chopped

500 g (1 lb 2 oz) potatoes, cut into quarters

6 cups gluten-free vegetable stock

1 cup milk

1 cup grated reduced-fat cheddar

⅓ cup grated parmesan

salt

freshly ground black pepper

Melt the butter in a large stockpot over medium–high heat. Add the cauliflower and potato and cook, stirring, for 3–4 minutes or until lightly golden. Add the vegetable stock and bring to the boil. Cook for 15–20 minutes, stirring occasionally.

Remove from the heat and leave to cool for 15 minutes. Use a hand-held blender to puree the vegetables to a smooth consistency (alternatively, place in a food processor and process until smooth). Stir in the milk and cheeses until evenly combined and the cheese has melted. Season to taste with salt and pepper.

◇ *Regular milk can be replaced with lactose-free milk.*

Split Pea and Bacon Soup

This is a real winter treat. Be aware though that this soup is not suitable for people with a dietary intolerance to raffinose, a complex carbohydrate found in peas, among other foods.

Serves 4–6

15 rashers lean bacon, diced

3 cloves garlic, crushed

1 large carrot, cut into 5 mm (¼ inch) cubes

2 potatoes, cut into 5 mm (¼ inch) cubes

1¼ cups dried green split peas, rinsed

6 cups gluten-free vegetable stock

salt

freshly ground black pepper

Heat a large heavy-based non-stick saucepan over medium heat. Add the bacon and garlic and cook, stirring, for 5 minutes.

Add the carrot, potato, split peas and vegetable stock to the pan. Bring to the boil, then reduce the heat and simmer gently, covered, for 1 hour or until the peas have become very soft. Stir occasionally during cooking.

Remove the lid and increase the heat to medium. Simmer for 15 minutes or until the soup has thickened slightly. Season to taste.

Gluten-free Lunch Boxes

It is essential that the school lunch box provides only suitable food, but it should still be fun!

It can sometimes seem difficult to balance good nutrition with good flavours, and gluten-free foods are no exception. Regular breads and rolls are usually made from wheat and/or rye, and therefore are not an option. This creates the first dilemma for parents!

A great range of gluten-free breads is now available such as white, grain, flatbreads and corn tortillas. Each of these breads offers a different taste – if your child does not like one style, try another, and you may find one that suits.

Gluten-free bread is often a little crumbly (gluten helps with elasticity and retaining moisture). One way around this is to store bread in the freezer at home and allow the bread to defrost in the lunch box. You may also make special arrangements with the teachers or tuckshop to allow your child to refresh bread in the microwave or use a toaster at school. For older children, try packing bread and fillings separately, and have your child make the sandwich at school.

Lunch swapping must be avoided for all children with food intolerances, and this must be relayed to the school. The simplest way to stop it, of course, is to make the lunches so delicious that your children won't want to give them away.

Gluten-free food to include in the lunch box

- Fresh or tinned fruit – whole, or cut up into pieces or made into kebabs

- Rice balls or arancini (see page 63)

- Vegetable sticks (such as carrot and capsicum sticks or cherry tomatoes) with gluten-free dip

- Cheese slices, cubes or sticks

- Gluten-free yoghurt

- Sandwiches made with gluten-free bread

- Boiled eggs

- Omelette wraps (see page 30)

- Gluten-free crispbreads or rice cakes topped with cold meat and cheese, ricotta or cream cheese spreads, or peanut butter (if permitted)

- Unsalted nuts (if permitted)

- Dried fruit or seeds (pumpkin or sunflower)

- Plain popcorn

- Salads

- Savoury muffins (see page 38)

- Soups

- Gluten-free pizzas (see page 30)

Sandwich Alternatives

- **Tandoori Chicken Omelette Wrap:** Heat some olive oil in a frying pan over medium heat. Add 300 g (10½ oz) sliced lean chicken and 2 tablespoons gluten-free tandoori paste and cook for 3–5 minutes or until cooked. Remove. Take 6 eggs. Heat a medium non-stick frying pan over medium heat and spray with non-stick spray. Crack 1 egg into a bowl, whisk then pour into the pan, rolling the pan to ensure the egg is spread evenly. Cook for 30–60 seconds, then flip gently with a spatula. Set aside to cool. Repeat with the remaining eggs to make 6 omelettes. Shred 1 cup of lettuce and cut 2 tomatoes into slices. Place the omelettes on a flat surface. Top with a row of chicken from the centre up to the top of the wrap, then add lettuce, sliced tomato and spread with natural yoghurt. Fold the bottom of the wrap into the centre. Roll from left to right, encasing the contents. *Makes 6*

- **Mini Hawaiian Pizzas:** Preheat the oven to 120°C (250°F). Line the baking trays with baking paper. Following the packet directions, prepare 2 cups of gluten-free bread mix. Using the back of a metal spoon, spread the bread mix over the baking trays to a thickness of 5 mm (¼ inch). Bake for 15 minutes, or until lightly browned. Remove from the oven, and increase the temperature to 180°C (350°F). Using a scone cutter, cut circles from the cooked base. Heat 2 teaspoons olive oil in a heavy-based frying pan over medium heat and cook 300 g (10½ oz) sliced bacon until crispy. Remove from the heat and stir in 200 g (7 oz) sliced gluten-free ham. Spread tomato paste and crushed garlic over each base. Top with the bacon and ham mixture, then divide a 420 g (15 oz) tin crushed pineapple among the pizzas. Finish with grated mozzarella. Bake for 15 minutes or until the cheese has melted. *Makes 20*

- **Fried Rice Noodle Cakes:** Break 375 g (13 oz) dried rice noodles into 5–10 cm (2–4 inch) pieces. Soak in hot water for 4–5 minutes. Drain, rinse and place in a large bowl. Heat a large frying pan over medium heat. Spray with non-stick spray, add 3 lightly beaten eggs and cook, stirring regularly. Remove. Add 200 g (7 oz) chopped bacon and cook until crispy. Remove the pan from the heat. Add the egg, ½ cup frozen pea and corn mix, 3 crushed cloves of garlic, 2 tablespoons sesame oil, ⅓ cup gluten-free soy sauce, 2 tablespoons gluten-free cornflour (cornstarch), salt and pepper to the noodles. Mix. Heat a heavy-based frying pan over medium heat. Spray the pan and some egg rings with non-stick spray. Put the rings in the pan. Spoon the noodle mixture into the rings and cook for 2–3 minutes each side. Run a knife around the inside of each ring to remove the cakes. *Makes 15–20*

- **Cheese and Herb Potato Tortilla:** Grease a 23 cm (9 inch) round baking dish. Melt 80 g (2¾ oz) butter in a non-stick frying pan over medium–high heat, add 2 crushed cloves of garlic and cook for 1–2 minutes or until golden. Reduce the heat to medium, add 1 kg (2 lb 4 oz) thinly sliced potatoes and season. Cook for 20 minutes or until tender, stirring the potatoes gently to ensure they cook evenly. Remove from the heat. Layer the potatoes in the baking dish. Preheat the oven to 180°C (350°F). Lightly beat 8 eggs, ½ cup chopped herbs (eg parsley, rosemary or thyme) and salt and pepper in a bowl. Pour the beaten egg over the potato, turning the dish to ensure the eggs are distributed well through the potato. Sprinkle with 3 tablespoons grated parmesan and bake for 15–20 minutes. Leave for 10 minutes before cutting into wedges. *Serves 6–8*

Afternoon Tea

Orange and Poppy Seed Biscuits

The winning flavour combination of orange and poppy seed is highlighted in these almond meal biscuits. If you fancy a change, lemon can easily be substituted.

Makes 20–25

1½ cups almond meal

¾ cup castor (superfine) sugar

⅓ cup fine rice flour

finely grated zest of 1 orange

2 tablespoons poppy seeds

2 eggs, separated

Preheat the oven to 140°C (275°F). Line two large baking trays with baking paper.

Place the almond meal, castor sugar, rice flour, orange zest and poppy seeds in a medium bowl and mix until well combined.

In a clean medium bowl, beat the egg whites until stiff peaks form, then fold gently into the almond mixture. Fold the egg yolks into the mixture.

Place rounded teaspoons of the mixture on the baking trays about 2 cm (¾ inch) apart. Bake for 20–25 minutes or until golden brown. Cool on the trays for 5 minutes, then transfer to a wire rack to cool completely.

Cheese and Corn Savoury Pikelets

These pikelets are simple to make and always delicious. They can also be used as a lunch-box filler or finger food or enjoyed as part of a relaxed Sunday brunch.

Makes 15–20

1 cup fine rice flour

½ cup soy flour

½ cup fine polenta

¾ teaspoon bicarbonate of soda

1 teaspoon xanthan gum (optional)

2 eggs, lightly beaten

1¼ cups milk

1 cup grated parmesan

1 cup tinned corn kernels, drained

½ cup grated zucchini (courgette) (optional)

40 g (1½ oz) butter, melted

Sift the flours, polenta, bicarbonate of soda and xanthan gum three times into a large bowl (or mix well with a whisk to ensure they are well combined). Combine the egg, milk, parmesan, corn and zucchini (if using) in a medium bowl. Pour into the dry ingredients and mix with a spoon until well combined. Stir in the melted butter, then leave to rest for 10 minutes.

Heat a large frying pan over low–medium heat for 2 minutes. Spray with non-stick spray, then pour in 2 tablespoons of batter for each pikelet.

Cook for 2–3 minutes or until bubbles start to appear. Flip over and cook for 2 minutes. Serve warm spread with butter or low-fat cream cheese.

◇ *Regular milk can be replaced with lactose-free milk.*

Pizza Muffins

The Italian flavours work really well together to make these a popular treat. Any muffins that don't disappear immediately can be frozen for another time.

Makes 12

170 g (6 oz) fine rice flour

75 g (2½ oz) gluten-free cornflour (cornstarch)

45 g (1½ oz) soy flour

2 teaspoons gluten-free baking powder

1 teaspoon bicarbonate of soda

1 teaspoon xanthan gum (optional)

3 eggs

160 g (5¾ oz) butter, melted

200 g (7 oz) gluten-free natural yoghurt

¾ cup milk

1 cup grated parmesan

2 tomatoes, diced

salt

freshly ground black pepper

2 tablespoons tomato paste

1 tablespoon mixed Italian herbs

½ cup grated cheddar

Preheat the oven to 170°C (325°F). Grease a 12-hole standard muffin tin.

Sift the flours, baking powder, bicarbonate of soda and xanthan gum three times into a large bowl (or mix well with a whisk to ensure they are well combined).

Place the eggs, melted butter, yoghurt, milk, parmesan and tomato in a medium bowl. Season with salt and pepper and stir until well combined. Add to the dry ingredients and beat well with a wooden spoon for 2–3 minutes.

Pour the mixture evenly into the muffin holes until about two-thirds full. Top with a dollop of tomato paste and a sprinkle of herbs and grated cheddar. Bake for 12–15 minutes or until firm to the touch and a skewer comes out clean when inserted into the centre of the muffin. Leave to stand for 5 minutes, then transfer to a wire rack to cool.

◇ *The yoghurt can be replaced with lactose-free yoghurt.*

Plain Sweet Biscuits

These versatile biscuits can be crushed to make biscuit bases for cheesecakes and slices. For a change, try adding 1–2 teaspoons of finely grated lemon or orange zest to the dough prior to baking.

Makes 20

90 g (3¼ oz) soy flour

150 g (5½ oz) gluten-free cornflour (cornstarch)

2 tablespoons desiccated coconut

2 teaspoons gluten-free baking powder

125 g (4½ oz) butter

2 teaspoons vanilla essence

165 g (5¾ oz) castor (superfine) sugar

1 egg

Preheat the oven to 180°C (350°F). Line two flat baking trays with baking paper.

Sift the flour, cornflour, coconut and baking powder three times into a medium bowl (or mix well with a whisk to ensure they are well combined).

Place the butter, vanilla essence, sugar and egg in a medium bowl and beat until smooth. Stir in the dry ingredients.

Roll out the dough between two sheets of baking paper. Cut into shapes with a biscuit cutter and lift onto the baking trays. Bake for 15 minutes or until golden brown. Leave to cool on the trays for 5 minutes, then transfer to a wire rack to cool completely.

Continental Spice Cake

This delectable cake can be served as a dessert with berry coulis (see page 126). You might find that the cake sags in the middle as it cooks but this in no way affects the flavour.

Serves 12

190 g (6¾ oz) butter, cubed

330 g (11½ oz) castor (superfine) sugar

2 teaspoons vanilla essence

3 eggs

90 g (3¼ oz) fine rice flour

30 g (1 oz) soy flour

3 tablespoons gluten-free cornflour (cornstarch)

1 teaspoon bicarbonate of soda

2 teaspoons gluten-free baking powder

1 teaspoon ground cinnamon

1 teaspoon xanthan gum (optional)

1 cup hazelnut meal

250 g (9 oz) reduced-fat sour cream

pure icing (confectioner's) sugar, for dusting

cream to serve (optional)

Preheat the oven to 170°C (325°F). Grease and line a 23 cm (9 inch) springform tin.

Place the butter, castor sugar and vanilla essence in a medium bowl and beat with electric beaters until thick, pale and creamy. Add the eggs, one at a time, beating well between each addition.

Sift the flours, bicarbonate of soda, baking powder, ground cinnamon and xanthan gum three times into a large bowl (or mix well with a whisk to ensure they are well combined). Stir in the hazelnut meal.

Using a large metal spoon, gently fold the dry ingredients into the butter mixture, alternating with the sour cream. Spoon the mixture into the tin and bake for 50–60 minutes or until a skewer comes out clean when inserted into the centre of the cake. Leave to cool in the tin for 10 minutes, then transfer to a wire rack to cool completely. Serve dusted with icing sugar and a dollop of cream, if desired.

Lamington Fingers

Lamingtons are real comfort food, aren't they? Here's a recipe for you in case you can't get your hands on a commercially prepared gluten-free version.

Makes 10

½ cup strawberry jam

1½ cups desiccated coconut

SPONGE

5 eggs

1 cup sugar

80 g (2¾ oz) fine rice flour

40 g (1½ oz) gluten-free custard powder

1 teaspoon xanthan gum (optional)

1 teaspoon gluten-free baking powder

ICING

3 cups pure icing (confectioner's) sugar

3 tablespoons cocoa powder

20 g (¾ oz) unsalted butter, melted

2 teaspoons vanilla essence

3 tablespoons boiling water

Preheat the oven to 180°C (350°F). Grease two 15 cm (6 inch) square sandwich tins.

To make the sponge, place the eggs in a large bowl and beat for 8 minutes or until thick and foamy. Beat in the sugar until dissolved.

Sift the flour, custard powder, xanthan gum and baking powder three times into a separate bowl (or mix well with a whisk to ensure they are well combined). Fold into the egg mixture with a metal spoon.

Pour into the sandwich tins and bake for 25 minutes or until the cakes spring back to the touch. Transfer to a wire rack and leave to cool.

To make the icing, sift the icing sugar and cocoa powder into a medium bowl. Add the butter, vanilla and water and mix until smooth.

Spread the jam over the top of one of the cooled cakes, then top with the other. Cut the cake into 10 fingers approximately 7.5 cm (3 inches) × 3 cm (1¼ inches). Dip the fingers into the chocolate icing, ensuring they are fully covered, then coat in desiccated coconut. Set aside on a wire rack to dry.

Cornbread

It's so worthwhile exploring bread alternatives on a gluten-free diet. I'm sure you will love this cornbread – I find it delicious toasted and topped with an olive spread.

Serves 10–12

115 g (4 oz) fine rice flour

45 g (1½ oz) tapioca flour

1 teaspoon xanthan gum (optional)

3½ teaspoons gluten-free baking powder

1 teaspoon salt

1 cup polenta

2 tablespoons castor (superfine) sugar

1 cup milk

3 tablespoons extra light olive oil

1 egg, lightly beaten

Preheat the oven to 220°C (425°F). Brush an 11 cm (4¼ inch) × 22 cm (8½ inch) loaf tin with olive oil. Lightly dust with gluten-free flour, shaking out any excess.

Sift the flours, xanthan gum, baking powder and salt three times into a large bowl (or mix well with a whisk to ensure they are well combined). Add the polenta, castor sugar, milk, olive oil and egg, and mix well.

Pour the mixture into the tin and bake for 25–30 minutes or until a skewer comes out clean when inserted into the centre of the loaf. Leave to cool in the tin for 5 minutes, then transfer to a wire rack to cool. Serve at room temperature or place under a grill and toast both sides.

◇ *Regular milk can be replaced with lactose-free milk.*

Double Choc Chip Cookies

Double Choc Chip Cookies

And here they are, the cookies we all just love to eat. You might want to think about making a double batch.

Makes 20–25

125 g (4½ oz) unsalted butter

3 tablespoons brown sugar

3 tablespoons castor (superfine) sugar

1 egg

1 teaspoon vanilla essence

110 g (3¾ oz) fine rice flour

75 g (2½ oz) gluten-free cornflour (cornstarch)

3 tablespoons soy flour

½ teaspoon bicarbonate of soda

3 tablespoons cocoa powder

200 g (7 oz) chocolate chips

Preheat the oven to 170°C (325°F). Line three flat baking trays with baking paper.

In a medium bowl, cream the butter and sugars with electric beaters. Add the egg and vanilla essence and beat well.

Sift the flours, bicarbonate of soda and cocoa powder three times into a bowl (or mix with a whisk to ensure they are well combined). Add to the butter mixture and beat well. Stir in the chocolate chips.

Place large tablespoons of the mixture on the baking trays. Bake for 8–10 minutes or until golden brown. Leave to cool on the trays for 5 minutes, then transfer to a wire rack to cool completely.

Chewy Cookies

The combination of dark chocolate, nuts and dried fruit works deliciously well to give these cookies a great taste and texture.

Makes 20–25

170 g (6 oz) fine rice flour

45 g (1½ oz) soy flour

75 g (2½ oz) gluten-free cornflour (cornstarch)

1 teaspoon bicarbonate of soda

100 g (3½ oz) unsalted butter

1 teaspoon vanilla essence

1¼ cups firmly packed brown sugar

1 egg

½ cup sultanas

½ cup walnuts, chopped

½ cup dark chocolate bits

Preheat the oven to 180°C (350°F). Line three flat baking trays with baking paper.

Sift the flours and bicarbonate of soda three times into a large bowl (or mix with a whisk to ensure they are well combined). Place the butter, vanilla essence, brown sugar and egg in a medium bowl and beat until smooth. Stir in the dry ingredients, sultanas, walnuts and chocolate bits.

Drop rounded tablespoons of the mixture onto the baking trays (allow room for spreading). Fork-press each biscuit to flatten slightly, then bake for 10 minutes, or until just starting to brown. Cool on the trays for 5 minutes, then transfer to a wire rack to cool completely.

Family Chocolate Cake

This is the failproof, all-purpose, loved-by-everyone kind of chocolate cake you just have to make. Top with chocolate icing (see page 43), or go a little richer with some commercial choc-nut spread. It tastes divine.

Serves 12

170 g (6 oz) fine rice flour

75 g (2½ oz) gluten-free cornflour (cornstarch)

90 g (3¼ oz) potato flour

70 g (2½ oz) cocoa powder

2 teaspoons gluten-free baking powder

1 teaspoon bicarbonate of soda

1 teaspoon xanthan gum (optional)

2 eggs

330 g (11½ oz) sugar

50 g (1¾ oz) butter, melted

200 g (7 oz) gluten-free vanilla yoghurt

⅔ cup reduced-fat milk

pure icing (confectioner's) sugar, for dusting (optional)

cream to serve (optional)

Preheat the oven to 170°C (325°F). Grease a 23 cm (9 inch) springform tin.

Sift the flours, cocoa powder, baking powder, bicarbonate of soda and xanthan gum three times into a large bowl (or mix well with a whisk to ensure they are well combined).

Place the eggs and sugar in a medium bowl and beat with electric beaters until thick and foamy. Add the melted butter, yoghurt and milk and stir until well combined. Add to the dry ingredients and beat with electric beaters for 2–3 minutes.

Pour the mixture into the tin and bake for 50–60 minutes or until firm to the touch and a skewer comes out clean when inserted into the centre of the cake. Leave to cool in the tin for 5 minutes, then transfer to a wire rack to cool completely. Lightly dust with icing sugar or top with chocolate icing before serving. Serve with cream, if desired.

◇ *The yoghurt can be replaced with lactose-free yoghurt.*

Banana Spice Muffins

Banana Spice Muffins

The enjoyment of these muffins starts with the wonderful aromas that fill the kitchen as they bake.

Makes 12

170 g (6 oz) fine rice flour

75 g (2½ oz) gluten-free cornflour (cornstarch)

90 g (3¼ oz) potato flour

1 teaspoon bicarbonate of soda

2 teaspoons gluten-free baking powder

1 teaspoon xanthan gum (optional)

2 teaspoons mixed spice

1 teaspoon ground cinnamon

40 g (1½ oz) butter, melted

200 g (7 oz) gluten-free vanilla yoghurt

2 eggs

2 ripe bananas, mashed

220 g (7¾ oz) sugar

Preheat the oven to 170°C (325°F). Grease a 12-hole standard muffin tin or line with patty cases.

Sift the flours, bicarbonate of soda, baking powder, xanthan gum and spices three times into a large bowl (or mix well with a whisk to ensure they are well combined).

Combine the melted butter, yoghurt and eggs, stir in the mashed banana and sugar, then add to the dry ingredients. Mix well with electric beaters for 2–3 minutes.

Pour the mixture evenly into the muffin holes until about two-thirds full and bake for 15–20 minutes or until golden brown and a skewer comes out clean when inserted into the centre of the muffin. Leave to stand for 5 minutes, then transfer to a wire rack to cool.

◆ *The yoghurt can be replaced with lactose-free yoghurt.*

Apricot Yoghurt Slice

Berry yoghurt works well in this recipe too – use pureed strawberries instead of the apricot nectar.

Serves 10–12

200 g (7 oz) packet plain gluten-free sweet biscuits

60 g (2¼ oz) butter, melted

3 tablespoons boiling water

1½ tablespoons powdered gelatine

500 g (1 lb 2 oz) gluten-free low-fat apricot yoghurt

3 tablespoons pure icing (confectioner's) sugar

3 tablespoons boiling water, extra

2 teaspoons powdered gelatine, extra

200 ml (7 fl oz) apricot nectar

Crush the biscuits into fine crumbs. Add the melted butter and mix until well combined. Press evenly into the base of a 20 cm (8 inch) x 30 cm (12 inch) lamington tin. Set aside.

Combine the boiling water and gelatine in a small heatproof bowl. Set the bowl over a larger bowl of boiling water and stir until the gelatine has completely dissolved.

Spoon the yoghurt into a medium bowl. Add the dissolved gelatine and stir until very well combined and smooth. Pour the yoghurt mixture over the biscuit base and chill in the refrigerator for at least 2 hours or until set.

Combine the extra boiling water and extra gelatine in a small heatproof bowl. Set the bowl over a larger bowl of boiling water and stir constantly until the gelatine has completely dissolved. Pour into the apricot nectar and stir until very well combined. Pour over the set yoghurt base to about 5 mm (¼ inch) thick. Return to the refrigerator for at least 2 hours or until set.

◆ *The yoghurt can be replaced with lactose-free yoghurt.*

Plate-free Food

Felafels

This is a variation on the usual method of making felafels, which is typically based on cracked wheat. The cashews, sunflower seeds and tahini make these a delicious, high-protein nibble that everyone can enjoy.

Makes 12–15

⅓ cup cashews

3 tablespoons sunflower seeds

3 tablespoons tahini

¾ cup fresh gluten-free breadcrumbs

1 egg, lightly beaten

3 tablespoons chopped parsley

2 cloves garlic, crushed

1 teaspoon sugar

2 tablespoons water

salt

freshly ground black pepper

olive oil, for frying

Preheat the oven to 150°C (300°F).

Place the cashews and sunflower seeds in a food processor and blend until finely ground. Transfer to a medium bowl, add the tahini, breadcrumbs, egg, parsley, garlic and sugar. Add a little water if the mixture is too dry. Taste and season with salt and pepper, and mix with a spoon or your hands until well combined. Shape into small patties, about 5 cm (2 inches) in diameter.

Heat the olive oil in a non-stick frying pan over medium heat. Add the felafels in batches and cook for 3–4 minutes each side or until golden brown. Transfer to a plate, cover with foil and keep warm in the oven while you make the remaining felafels.

Rice Paper Rolls

If you feel like a change, the recipe also works well with chicken or tofu instead of prawns.

Makes 18–20

100 g (3½ oz) vermicelli noodles

1 packet round rice paper sheets (22 cm/8 inch diameter)

1½ cups finely shredded lettuce

200 g (7 oz) cooked prawns (shrimp), peeled

1 small carrot, cut into thin 3 cm (1¼ inch) strips

100 g (3½ oz) snow peas (mange-tout), thinly sliced

½ cup finely chopped coriander (cilantro) leaves

3 tablespoons gluten-free hoisin sauce

DIPPING SAUCE

3 tablespoons gluten-free sweet chilli sauce

2 tablespoons brown sugar

3 tablespoons rice wine vinegar

2 tablespoons lime juice

salt

Break the noodles into 10 cm (4 inch) pieces, then soak in a large bowl of hot water for 4–5 minutes or until softened. Rinse under cold water; drain well.

Fill a large flat dish with hot water. Soak a rice paper sheet in the water for 1 minute to soften. Blot dry on paper towel. Place a small handful of noodles, 2 tablespoons lettuce, a prawn and pieces of carrot and snow pea in a line on the bottom third of the rice paper sheet. Top with coriander and a drizzle of hoisin sauce. Roll over once and fold in the edges. Continue to roll up tightly. Cover with a moist cloth while you make the rest of the rolls.

To make the dipping sauce, combine all the ingredients in a bowl and mix well. Serve with the rice paper rolls.

Thai Chicken Skewers

Thai Chicken Skewers

This is such an easy dish to prepare. The skewers are fantastic as finger food, but can also be served as a starter on a bed of jasmine rice.

Makes 12

2 tablespoons chopped lemongrass

¼ cup chopped coriander (cilantro) leaves

1 tablespoon fish sauce

2 teaspoons sweet chilli sauce

2 tablespoons sesame oil

3 cloves garlic, crushed

2 teaspoons coconut essence

600 g (1 lb 5 oz) skinless chicken breast, cut into
    2 cm (¾ inch) strips

12 wooden skewers

lime wedges, to serve (optional)

Combine the lemongrass, coriander, fish sauce, sweet chilli sauce, sesame oil, garlic and coconut essence in a large bowl. Add the chicken strips and toss to coat in the marinade. Cover and refrigerate for 2 hours.

Soak the wooden skewers in water for 10 minutes to prevent scorching.

Preheat a grill plate, chargrill pan or barbecue grill to medium–high. Thread the marinated chicken strips onto the skewers and cook for 5–10 minutes or until just cooked through. Serve with lime wedges.

Chicken Nuggets

This popular little bite is rarely available gluten-free. When you're preparing these, why not make an extra batch and freeze them for next time?

Makes about 50

3 tablespoons gluten-free cornflour (cornstarch)

2 eggs, lightly beaten

½ cup gluten-free breadcrumbs

400 g (14 oz) skinless chicken breast, cut into
    2 cm (¾ inch) cubes

vegetable oil, for drizzling (optional)

prepared gluten-free sweet chilli sauce or tomato sauce,
    to serve

Preheat the oven to 180°C (350°F). Spray a baking tray with non-stick spray.

Set out three shallow bowls: put the cornflour in one, the beaten egg in another, and the breadcrumbs in the final bowl. Coat the chicken pieces in the cornflour, dip them in the egg, then toss them in the breadcrumbs.

Place the chicken pieces on the baking tray and drizzle with oil (if using). Bake for 10 minutes; turn once, then bake for a further 5 minutes or until the chicken is cooked. Serve with sweet chilli sauce or tomato sauce.

Middle Eastern Meatballs

Tasty bite-size balls that are easy to prepare and packed to the brim with flavour. Always a popular choice.

Makes about 50

650 g (1 lb 7 oz) minced (ground) beef

½ teaspoon chilli powder, or to taste

1½ tablespoons cumin seeds

1 tablespoon ground cumin

½ cup almond meal

⅓ cup tomato paste

2 eggs

salt

freshly ground black pepper

Preheat the oven to 180°C (350°F).

Combine the minced beef, chilli, cumin seeds, ground cumin, almond meal, tomato paste and eggs in a large bowl. Season well with salt and pepper.

Shape the mixture into small balls about the size of a walnut (you should have enough to make about 50 meatballs).

Place the meatballs on a baking tray and cover with foil. Bake for 20 minutes or until cooked through.

Mini Fish Cakes with Lime Dipping Sauce

These can be shaped to look like baby muffins (as pictured), or just roll them into small balls and bake in the muffin tin or on a flat tray.

Makes 12–15

3 cloves garlic, crushed

2 teaspoons sesame oil

1 teaspoon chopped lemongrass

1 teaspoon seeded and chopped fresh red chilli

1 tablespoon chopped ginger

2 tablespoons fish sauce

1 egg, beaten

2 tablespoons chopped coriander (cilantro) leaves

415 g (14¾ oz) tin salmon

DIPPING SAUCE

½ cup rice wine vinegar

3 tablespoons sugar

2 tablespoons lime juice

1 large fresh red chilli, seeded and finely sliced

Preheat the oven to 180°C (350°F). Spray one or two mini-muffin tins with non-stick spray.

Place the garlic, sesame oil, lemongrass, chilli, ginger, fish sauce, egg, coriander and salmon in the bowl of a food processor and process until well combined.

Spoon the mixture into the mini-muffin holes and bake for 10–15 minutes or until cooked through and golden brown.

To make the dipping sauce, place all the ingredients in a bowl and mix well. Serve with the fish cakes.

Mini Fish Cakes with Lime Dipping Sauce

Indian Vegetable Fritters

Besan flour is made from chickpeas. The aromatic spices of cumin and coriander complement the nutty flavour of the flour perfectly.

Serves 10–12

SPICED YOGHURT
200 g (7 oz) low-fat natural yoghurt
1 tablespoon ground cumin
1½ teaspoons ground coriander
½ teaspoon turmeric

VEGETABLE FRITTERS
75 g (2½ oz) gluten-free cornflour (cornstarch)
75 g (2½ oz) besan flour (or soy flour)
1 teaspoon baking powder
2 tablespoons ground cumin
3 teaspoons ground coriander
1 teaspoon turmeric

salt
freshly ground black pepper
3 eggs
200 g (7 oz) low-fat natural yoghurt
vegetable oil, for frying
250 g (9 oz) cauliflower, cut into small florets
1 zucchini (courgette), cut into
    5 mm (¼ inch) thick slices
200 g (7 oz) pumpkin, cut into
    5 mm (¼ inch) thick slices
½ eggplant (aubergine), cut into
    5 mm (¼ inch) thick slices

Preheat the oven to 140°C (275°F).

To make the spiced yoghurt, place all the ingredients in a small bowl and mix well. Set aside while you make the fritters.

Sift the flours, baking powder and spices into a large bowl. Season with salt and pepper.

Beat the eggs and yoghurt together in a small bowl. Add the mixture to the dry ingredients and beat until well combined.

Heat 3 cm (1¼ inch) oil in a large saucepan or wok over medium heat until hot.

Dip the cauliflower, zucchini, pumpkin and eggplant into the batter, four pieces at a time. Place gently in the hot oil and cook, turning twice, for 2–3 minutes or until golden.

Remove with a slotted spoon and drain on paper towels. Transfer to a baking tray and keep warm in the oven while you cook the rest of the vegetables. Serve with the spiced yoghurt.

◆ *The yoghurt can be replaced with lactose-free yoghurt.*

Avocado and Corn Dip

The simplicity of this recipe is great. Perfect as a dip, it also works well as a spread on gluten-free crispbreads, topped with chicken or ham.

Serves 6–8

2 ripe avocados

3 tablespoons low-fat sour cream

½ cup gluten-free creamed corn

¼ teaspoon cayenne pepper

corn chips or vegetable sticks, to serve

Mash the avocado with a fork to make a smooth paste. Add the sour cream, corn and cayenne pepper and mix together well. Serve with corn chips or vegetable sticks.

◇ *If you are lactose intolerant, this dip should be consumed in small quantities.*

Tuna and Ricotta Dip

I often whip this one up and serve it to friends – it's a real crowd pleaser.

Serves 6–8

425 g (15 oz) tin tuna in brine, drained

400 g (14 oz) fresh ricotta

1 tablespoon lemon juice

1 tablespoon whole-egg mayonnaise

½ teaspoon chilli powder

1 tablespoon chopped parsley

vegetable sticks, to serve

Combine all the ingredients in a large bowl. Use a hand-held blender to process until well combined.

Serve with freshly cut sticks of carrot, celery, cucumber and capsicum (pepper).

◇ *If you are lactose intolerant, this dip should be consumed in small quantities.*

Spinach and Fetta Arancini

Arancini are an Italian classic. The base recipe can be adapted to work with many flavour variations but I just love the delicious combination of spinach, fetta and pine nuts.

Makes about 30

2 cups white rice

2 eggs, lightly beaten

125 g (4½ oz) chopped cooked spinach

1 cup grated parmesan

100 g (3½ oz) soft fetta, crumbled

3 tablespoons pine nuts, toasted

salt

freshly ground black pepper

⅔ cup maize cornflour (cornstarch)

2 eggs, lightly beaten, extra

1½ cups gluten-free breadcrumbs

vegetable oil, for frying

lemon wedges and shaved parmesan, to serve (optional)

Preheat the oven to 150°C (300°F).

Cook the rice as per packet instructions. Remove from the heat and allow to cool to room temperature.

Place the cooled rice, egg, spinach, parmesan, fetta and pine nuts in a large bowl and mix together well. Season to taste. Roll the mixture into balls a little larger than a golf ball. Chill in the refrigerator for at least 1 hour.

Set out three shallow bowls: put the cornflour in one, the extra beaten egg in another, and the breadcrumbs in the final bowl. Roll the balls in the cornflour to lightly coat, dip them in the egg, then toss them in the breadcrumbs to coat. Place the balls on a baking tray.

Half-fill a deep-fryer or large heavy-based saucepan with vegetable oil and heat to 190°C (375°F) – the oil is hot enough when a cube of bread browns in 15 seconds. Add 3–4 balls at a time and cook for 3–4 minutes or until golden brown. Remove with a slotted spoon and drain on paper towels. Transfer to a baking tray and keep warm in the oven while you cook the rest of the arancini. Serve warm with lemon wedges and shaved parmesan, if desired.

Drinks

This book would not be complete without a few ideas to help quench the thirst – so I've included a few of my favourite recipes for non-alcoholic drinks.

But what about alcoholic drinks? Alcohol should always be enjoyed in moderation, but it is great to know it can still be enjoyed gluten-free. And aren't we lucky that there are so many types of drinks to choose from: wine, champagne, most spirits and liqueurs. There's also been an exciting development on the beer front. While regular beer, stout, ale and lagers contain gluten, it is now possible to buy gluten-free beer. It might be difficult to seek out, but those who have tried it think it's worth the effort!

Pink Lemonade: In a medium saucepan, heat 10 cups water, 2½ cups castor (superfine) sugar and 2½ cups fresh lemon juice over low heat, stirring regularly until the sugar has dissolved. Remove from the heat and stir in ½ cup cranberry juice. Leave to cool to room temperature, then place in the refrigerator to cool completely. Serve over ice. *Serves 8–10*

Pine Orange Tango: Using a vegetable peeler, remove the zest from 2 oranges in long strips. Squeeze the juice. Place the orange zest and juice, 1 cup water, 150 ml (5 fl oz) pineapple juice and 1½ tablespoons sugar in a medium saucepan over low heat and stir regularly until the sugar has dissolved. Remove from the heat and leave to cool to room temperature. Remove the orange zest. Stir in 1 cup low-fat milk and ¼ teaspoon vanilla essence, then place in the refrigerator to cool completely. Serve over ice. *Serves 4*

Grapefruit Cool: Wash, hull and halve 8 strawberries and cut 4 limes into wedges. Divide the strawberries, lime wedges and 2 tablespoons crushed ice among 4 glasses. Pour ½ cup pink grapefruit juice into each glass and top with ½ cup diet lemonade. *Serves 4*

Very Berry Smoothie: Place 250 g (9 oz) strawberries, 200 g (7 oz) raspberries and 400 g (14 oz) low-fat strawberry yoghurt in a blender and blend until smooth (or alternatively, use a hand-held blender). Stir in 1 cup crushed ice and pour into glasses. *Serves 4*

Nutty Chocnana Smoothie: Place 1 ripe banana, 2 tablespoons gluten-free powdered drinking chocolate, 2 tablespoons smooth peanut butter, 2 tablespoons castor (superfine) sugar and 400 ml (14 fl oz) skim milk in a blender and blend until smooth. Add more peanut butter or drinking chocolate if desired. *Serves 2*

Berry Slush: Place 1 cup water, ½ cup sugar and 3 tablespoons lemon juice in small saucepan over low heat and stir regularly until the sugar has dissolved. Leave to cool to room temperature, then place the sugar mixture, 500 g (1 lb 2 oz) strawberries and 200 g (7 oz) blueberries in a blender and blend until smooth (or alternatively, use a hand-held blender). Pour the berry mixture into a shallow freezer-proof container and place in the freezer for 3–4 hours or until almost frozen. Scoop out of the container and serve immediately. *Serves 4*

◇ *The regular milk and yoghurt in the Pine Orange Tango and the smoothie recipes can be replaced with lactose-free milk and yoghurt.*

Dinners

Paprika Chicken

People who don't have a lot of confidence in the kitchen will love this recipe. It is simple to prepare, the ingredients are easy to find and the taste is just fantastic. Serve with steamed rice and a healthy green salad.

Serves 4

⅓ cup lemon juice

⅓ cup olive oil

1½ tablespoons sweet paprika

2 teaspoons cayenne pepper

2 tablespoons dried oregano

1½ tablespoons brown sugar

4 cloves garlic, crushed

1 small fresh red chilli, seeded and finely chopped

salt

freshly ground black pepper

4 pieces skinless chicken maryland

Combine the lemon juice, olive oil, paprika, cayenne pepper, oregano, brown sugar, garlic, chilli, salt and pepper in a small bowl.

Place the chicken pieces in a baking dish. Pour the paprika mixture over the chicken and toss well to coat. Cover with plastic film and leave to marinate in the refrigerator for at least 3 hours. Turn the chicken every hour to ensure it is well coated.

Preheat the oven to 200°C (400°F).

Bake the chicken pieces for 40 minutes or until the juices run clear when a skewer is inserted into the thickest part. Cover and leave to rest for 5 minutes before serving.

Roast Lamb Racks

How many of us love a great-tasting and succulent roast? Infused with flavoursome herbs, these racks are a great way to serve roast lamb. This dish goes well with traditional roast vegies.

Serves 4

1 tablespoon dried oregano

2 tablespoons dried parsley

2 teaspoons dried rosemary

2 cloves garlic, crushed

2 tablespoons olive oil

salt

freshly ground black pepper

2 racks of 8 lamb cutlets, trimmed of fat

Preheat the oven to 180°C (350°F).

Combine the dried herbs, garlic, olive oil, salt and pepper in a small bowl.

Rub the herb mixture over the lamb cutlets. Place in a baking dish and bake for 30 minutes or until the lamb is medium–rare.

Cut each rack in half and serve.

Roast Lamb Racks

Squid Stuffed with Garlic Prawn Risotto

This dish is fun to prepare and wonderful to eat. It can be quite filling though, so take care not to overstuff the squid.

Serves 6

6 cups gluten-free vegetable stock

1 tablespoon olive oil

6 cloves garlic, crushed

2 cups arborio rice

500 g (1 lb 2 oz) prawns (shrimp),
   peeled and deveined

⅓ cup reduced-fat cream

⅓ cup chopped parsley

salt

freshly ground black pepper

6 × 200 g (7 oz) squid bodies (tubes)

2 tablespoons olive oil, extra

NAPOLITANA SAUCE

1 × 400 g (14 oz) tin crushed tomatoes

½ cup reduced-fat cream

1 clove garlic, crushed

2 tablespoons chopped parsley

Heat the vegetable stock in a medium saucepan, then cover and keep at a gentle simmer over low heat.

Heat the olive oil in a large saucepan over medium heat. Add the garlic and cook for 1–2 minutes or until golden. Add the rice and stir to coat with the oil and garlic mixture.

Add 1 cup of the hot stock and stir until it is completely absorbed. Repeat this process, adding ½ cup of stock at a time until all but the last ½ cup of stock has been added. Stir in the prawns, cream and parsley, then add the last ½ cup of stock (if needed), stirring until completely absorbed. Season to taste with salt and pepper.

Spoon the mixture into the squid bodies (do not overfill) and seal with a toothpick at each end. Heat the extra olive oil in a large frying pan and cook the squid over medium heat until browned on all sides. Remove from the pan, cover and keep warm.

To make the napolitana sauce, combine all the ingredients in the frying pan used for the squid and stir gently over medium–low heat until the sauce comes to a simmer. Simmer gently for 10 minutes, then remove from the heat. Season to taste. Spoon the sauce onto serving plates. Cut the squid into slices and arrange on top.

Fish in Beer Batter

Fish in Beer Batter

Oh joy! Gluten-free beer is now available! It is a thrill to include a recipe for beer batter – I really hope you enjoy it.

Serves 4

400 g (14 oz) frozen gluten-free potato chips

¾ cup fine rice flour

1½ cups gluten-free cornflour (cornstarch)

salt

freshly ground black pepper

1⅓ cups gluten-free beer, chilled

sunflower oil, for deep-frying

12 × 50 g (1¾ oz) white fish fillets (eg flathead)

gluten-free cornflour (cornstarch), extra, for dusting

2 lemons, cut into wedges

prepared gluten-free tartare sauce, to serve

Bake the potato chips according to the packet instructions.

Sift the flours, 1 teaspoon salt and some pepper three times into a large bowl (or mix well with a whisk to ensure they are well combined). Make a well in the centre. Slowly add the beer and whisk to form a smooth batter.

Half-fill a deep-fryer or large heavy-based saucepan with sunflower oil and heat to 190°C (375°F) – the oil is hot enough when a cube of bread browns in 15 seconds.

Dust the fish fillets in the extra cornflour, then dip in the batter, one at a time, allowing any excess batter to drain off. Holding the tail, gently lower the fish into the oil; when the head end rises to the surface, let go of the fillet. This will prevent the fish from sticking to the side of the pan. Cook the fish in batches for 3–4 minutes or until golden brown and crisp. Drain on paper towels.

Season the fish with salt and serve with hot chips, lemon wedges and tartare sauce.

Pasta and Meatballs

Porcupine balls are a family favourite. In this recipe I have added my own twist with the addition of parmesan.

Serves 4

750 g (1 lb 10 oz) lean minced (ground) beef

1½ cups cooked long-grain rice

¾ cup grated parmesan

1 egg, beaten

2 cloves garlic, crushed

3 tablespoons chopped parsley

½ teaspoon cayenne pepper

salt

freshly ground black pepper

2 cups prepared gluten-free tomato soup

500 g (1 lb 2 oz) gluten-free penne pasta

grated parmesan, extra, to serve

Preheat the oven to 180°C (350°F).

Combine the minced beef, cooked rice, parmesan, egg, garlic, parsley and cayenne pepper in a large bowl and season well with salt and pepper. Shape into 16 balls.

Place the meatballs in a large casserole dish and cover with the tomato soup. Bake for 40–50 minutes or until the meatballs are cooked through.

Cook the pasta in a large saucepan of boiling water for 10–12 minutes or until al dente.

Spoon the meatballs over the pasta and serve with extra parmesan, if desired.

Chicken and Mushroom Casserole

Served with creamy mash, this is a hearty and nutritious family meal. If you feel like a change, use beef or pork instead of the chicken.

Serves 6

¼ cup gluten-free cornflour (cornstarch)

2 teaspoons smoked paprika

salt

freshly ground black pepper

1.5 kg (3 lb 5 oz) chicken thigh fillets, diced

2 teaspoons olive oil

2 cloves garlic, crushed

1 stalk celery, sliced

3 carrots, sliced

250 g (9 oz) button mushrooms, cut into quarters

410 g (14½ oz) tin crushed tomatoes

½ cup pureed tomato (passata)

3 potatoes, diced

140 g (5 oz) baby spinach leaves

1½ cups gluten-free chicken stock

Preheat the oven to 180°C (350°F).

Place the cornflour, paprika, salt and pepper in a small bowl and mix well. Transfer the seasoned flour to a plastic bag, add the chicken pieces and toss until well coated.

Heat the olive oil in a large saucepan over medium heat, add the garlic, celery, carrot and mushrooms and cook until the celery is golden brown. Stir in the crushed tomatoes, pureed tomato, potato, spinach and chicken stock and heat gently for 1–2 minutes.

Remove from the heat and add the seasoned chicken pieces. Transfer the mixture to an 8-cup ovenproof dish and bake, covered, for about 50 minutes. Check that the chicken pieces are cooked through and cook for longer if necessary. Season with salt and pepper.

Chow Mein

Chow Mein

This dish is easy to eat and tastes even better the next day. Make sure you leave plenty of leftovers!

Serves 4

200 g (7 oz) mung bean vermicelli (glass) noodles

1 tablespoon canola oil

3 cups finely chopped savoy or Chinese cabbage

4 stalks celery, sliced

2 carrots, diced

100 g (3½ oz) button mushrooms, sliced

2 cloves garlic, crushed

1 tablespoon chopped ginger

1 tablespoon gluten-free curry powder

500 g (1 lb 2 oz) lean minced (ground) beef

1 tablespoon gluten-free soy sauce

2 cups gluten-free beef stock

2 tablespoons gluten-free cornflour (cornstarch)

Break the noodles into 2–3 cm (1 inch) lengths, then soak in a large bowl of boiling water for 4–5 minutes or until softened. Drain and set aside.

Heat 2 teaspoons canola oil in a large non-stick frying pan over medium heat. Stir-fry the cabbage, celery, carrot and mushrooms for 6–8 minutes or until tender. Remove.

Heat the remaining oil in the pan. Add the garlic, ginger and curry powder and stir over medium heat for 2 minutes or until fragrant. Add the minced beef and stir until cooked.

Combine the soy sauce, beef stock and cornflour in a small bowl. Pour over the beef, return the vegetables and soaked noodles to the pan and stir until the sauce has thickened. Reduce the heat to low and simmer for 20–30 minutes. Stir regularly to prevent the mixture from sticking to the pan.

Tuna Mornay

My mum always made this so well when I was a kid. Tuna mornay is one of my real comfort foods – I'm sure it's the same for many of us.

Serves 6

2 cups long-grain rice

⅓ cup gluten-free cornflour (cornstarch)

2¼ cups reduced-fat milk

⅓ cup grated parmesan

2 cups grated reduced-fat cheddar

425 g (15 oz) tin tuna, drained

salt

freshly ground black pepper

Cook the rice as per packet instructions, then set aside.

In a small bowl, combine the cornflour with 3 tablespoons milk to form a paste. Add the remaining milk and mix well to ensure there are no lumps. Pour into a medium saucepan and stir constantly over medium heat until thickened. Do not boil.

Add the grated cheeses and tuna and stir until the cheese has melted. Season to taste and serve with the rice.

❖ *The milk can be replaced with lactose-free milk.*

Filet Mignon

You have probably seen filet mignon on restaurant menus many times, and now here is your chance to prepare this old-time favourite yourself.

Serves 4

1 tablespoon olive oil

1 tablespoon lemon juice

1 clove garlic, crushed

salt

freshly ground black pepper

4 × 180 g (6½ oz) fillet steaks

4 long rashers bacon, trimmed

SAUCE

⅓ cup cream

1½ tablespoons gluten-free Worcestershire sauce

1 tablespoon chopped parsley

1 teaspoon olive oil

1 clove garlic, crushed

Combine the olive oil, lemon juice, garlic, salt and pepper in a small bowl. Place the steaks in a baking dish, pour on the marinade and toss to coat. Cover with plastic film and marinate in the refrigerator for at least 3 hours.

Preheat the oven to 180°C (350°F).

Wrap a bacon rasher around each steak and hold in place with a toothpick. Heat a medium frying pan over medium–high heat, add the steaks and brown on both sides, turning to cook the bacon slightly. Transfer to a baking tray, cover with foil and bake for 15–20 minutes or until cooked to your liking. Cover and leave to rest while you make the sauce.

To make the sauce, combine the cream, Worcestershire sauce and parsley in a small bowl. Heat the oil in a medium frying pan, add the garlic and cook over medium–high heat for 1–2 minutes or until lightly browned. Add the cream mixture and meat juices from the baking dish and stir over the heat until the sauce thickens slightly. Season with salt and pepper and spoon over the steaks. Serve with vegetables and roughly mashed potatoes.

Cheese and Bacon Pasta Bake

There are many variations of pasta bakes. This one uses gluten-free pasta, so take care not to overcook it in the saucepan. It does get a second go in the oven.

Serves 4

400 g (14 oz) gluten-free macaroni

200 g (7 oz) bacon, trimmed and diced

⅓ cup gluten-free cornflour (cornstarch)

2¼ cups reduced-fat milk

2 cups grated reduced-fat cheddar

3 tablespoons tomato sauce

salt

freshly ground black pepper

½ cup gluten-free breadcrumbs

½ cup grated reduced-fat cheddar, extra

Preheat the oven to 180°C (350°F). Grease four 12 cm (4½ inch) baking dishes.

Bring a large saucepan of water to the boil and cook the macaroni as per packet instructions. When al dente, drain and return to the pan. Cover to keep warm.

Sauté the bacon pieces in a small non-stick frying pan over medium heat until crispy. Set aside.

In a small bowl, combine the cornflour with 3 tablespoons milk to form a paste. Add the remaining milk and mix well to ensure there are no lumps. Pour into a medium saucepan and stir constantly over medium heat until thickened. Do not boil. Add the grated cheddar, tomato sauce and bacon, and stir until the cheese has melted. Add the pasta, and stir until well combined. Season to taste with salt and pepper.

Pour into the baking dishes and sprinkle evenly with the combined breadcrumbs and extra cheddar. Bake for 20 minutes or until golden brown.

◇ *The milk can be replaced with lactose-free milk.*

Speedy Risotto

This quick-cooking adaptation of a traditional risotto means you can enjoy the flavour and texture of perfect risotto in minutes.

Serves 4

2 teaspoons olive oil

3 cloves garlic, crushed

400 g (14 oz) skinless chicken breast, sliced

6 cups gluten-free chicken stock

2 cups arborio rice

½ cup grated carrot

½ cup broccoli, cut into small florets

1 zucchini (courgette), cut in half and sliced

½ cup grated parmesan

3 tablespoons chopped parsley

salt

freshly ground black pepper

Heat the olive oil in a large non-stick frying pan over medium–high heat, add the garlic and chicken and cook for 3–5 minutes or until golden brown.

Pour the chicken stock into a large saucepan and bring to the boil. Add the rice and cook over medium–low heat, stirring continuously. When almost all of the liquid has been absorbed, add the chicken, carrot, broccoli and zucchini and stir until well combined. Continue cooking until all the liquid has been absorbed and the vegetables are tender. Add extra stock if required.

Stir in the parmesan and parsley, and season with salt and pepper. Serve immediately.

Peppered Veal Steaks

Marinating the meat is an important step in this recipe. Not only does it help tenderise the meat, it infuses it with delicious flavours that complete this simple dish.

Serves 4

3 cloves garlic, crushed

2 tablespoons lemon juice

1 tablespoon olive oil

2 tablespoons ground coriander

1 tablespoon coarsely ground black pepper

salt

4 x 200 g (7 oz) lean veal steaks

1 tablespoon olive oil, extra

Combine the garlic, lemon juice, olive oil, coriander, pepper and a little salt in a small bowl. Put the veal steaks in a plastic bag, add the garlic mixture and toss well to coat. Leave to marinate in the refrigerator for 3 hours.

Heat the extra olive oil in a large frying pan over medium heat. Add the steaks and cook for 4–5 minutes each side, or until cooked to your liking.

Pork Spare Ribs

It's not often we might think about making spare ribs at home, but this recipe should change all that. Now you can enjoy them, gluten-free, any time you like. Serve with hot chips and salad.

Serves 4

2–3 teaspoons gluten-free cornflour (cornstarch)

½ cup water

3 tablespoons sherry

⅓ cup gluten-free soy sauce

2 tablespoons gluten-free oyster sauce

3 whole star anise

1 tablespoon brown sugar

2 tablespoons sesame oil

3 cloves garlic, crushed

2–3 teaspoons finely chopped ginger

2 kg (4 lb 8 oz) pork spare ribs

Place the cornflour in a medium bowl and combine with a little water to form a paste. Add the sherry, soy sauce, oyster sauce, star anise, brown sugar and remaining water.

Heat the sesame oil in a medium saucepan over high heat. Add the garlic and ginger and cook for 1–2 minutes or until fragrant. Pour the sherry mixture into the pan and bring almost to boil, stirring continuously, until the sauce is thick enough to coat the back of a spoon. Remove from the heat and leave to cool to room temperature. Remove the star anise.

Brush the cooled sauce evenly over the pork spare ribs, making sure they are well coated. Cover and refrigerate for at least 3 hours.

Preheat the oven to 180°C (350°F). Place the ribs on a rack in an ovenproof dish and bake for 50–60 minutes or until cooked through.

Pork Spare Ribs

Chicken Fillet with Tarragon Mustard Sauce and Creamy Polenta

With its distinctive flavour, tarragon works really well with mustard, and the two complement the chicken perfectly.

Serves 4

2 tablespoons olive oil

1 clove garlic, crushed

4 × 150 g (5½ oz) skinless chicken breasts

CREAMY POLENTA

3 cups reduced-fat milk

2 cloves garlic, crushed

⅔ cup instant polenta

salt

freshly ground black pepper

TARRAGON MUSTARD SAUCE

2 tablespoons olive oil

1 clove garlic, crushed

3 tablespoons reduced-fat cream

3 tablespoons chopped tarragon

3 tablespoons Dijon mustard

1 tablespoon lemon juice

To make the creamy polenta, heat the milk and garlic in a medium saucepan until almost boiling. Add the polenta and stir until the mixture boils. Reduce the heat to low and stir constantly for a further 8–10 minutes or until the polenta is cooked (it should be the texture of mashed potato). Season with salt and pepper. Cover and keep warm.

Heat a little olive oil in a large frying pan over medium–low heat, add the garlic and cook for 1–2 minutes or until lightly browned. Add the remaining olive oil and cook the chicken breasts for 3–5 minutes each side, or until just cooked and golden brown. Cover and leave to rest while you make the sauce.

To make the sauce, heat the olive oil in a small frying pan over medium heat, add the garlic and cook until golden brown. Stir in the cream, tarragon, mustard and lemon juice and simmer for 3–5 minutes or until thickened slightly. Season to taste, then pour the sauce over the chicken and serve with creamy polenta.

◆ *The milk can be replaced with lactose-free milk.*

Paella

Paella is a wonderful dish, full of exciting flavours, textures and aromas. The wide variety of ingredients means that each mouthful offers something new.

Serves 6

1 tablespoon olive oil

100 g (3½ oz) gluten-free chorizo sausage, sliced

2 cloves garlic, crushed

1 red capsicum (pepper), seeded and sliced

1½ cups medium-grain white rice

¼ teaspoon turmeric

¼ teaspoon powdered saffron

3 cups gluten-free vegetable stock

2 tablespoons fish sauce

400 g (14 oz) tin crushed tomatoes

500 g (1 lb 2 oz) gluten-free marinara mix

300 g (10½ oz) firm white fish fillets, chopped

1 cup frozen peas

2 tablespoons olive oil, extra

Heat the olive oil in a large non-stick frying pan over medium heat. Add the chorizo and garlic and cook, stirring, until browned.

Reduce the heat to low, add the capsicum, rice, turmeric and saffron and cook, stirring, for 1–2 minutes. Stir in the vegetable stock, fish sauce and tomatoes. Simmer gently for 20 minutes.

Arrange the marinara mix, fish pieces and peas over the top of the rice mixture and cook, covered, over low heat for 6–10 minutes or until the rice is tender and the seafood is cooked through. Finish by stirring through the extra olive oil.

Lemongrass Snapper

I first made this dish with some snapper I caught in the Bay of Islands in New Zealand. I threw together these basic ingredients and the result was just divine. Make sure you only use fresh fish fillets. This dish goes best with steamed rice and vegetables.

Serves 4

2 tablespoons chopped lemongrass

½ cup chopped coriander (cilantro) leaves

2 small fresh red chillies, seeded and finely chopped

1 tablespoon sesame oil

2 cloves garlic, crushed

2 teaspoons grated ginger

2 tablespoons lime juice

salt

freshly ground black pepper

4 × 200 g (7 oz) snapper fillets

Place the lemongrass, coriander, chilli, sesame oil, garlic, ginger, lime juice, salt and pepper in a food processor and process to form a paste (you could also use a mortar and pestle).

Put the snapper fillets in a plastic bag, add the lemongrass paste and toss the fillets in the bag until evenly coated with the paste.

Preheat a grill plate, chargrill pan or barbecue grill to high. Cook the fillets for 3–4 minutes each side or until cooked through.

Beef and Black Bean Stir-fry

Fermented black beans are available from Asian grocers. Blackbean paste can be used, but it is worth taking the trouble to crush the beans yourself.

Serves 4

1 cup long-grain white rice

2 tablespoons sesame oil

1 clove garlic, crushed

¼ teaspoon grated ginger

¼ teaspoon finely chopped fresh red chilli

400 g (14 oz) beef steak, cut into 2.5 cm (1 inch) strips

1 bunch bok choy (pak choi), trimmed

125 g (4½ oz) snow peas (mange-tout), topped and tailed

125 g (4½ oz) mushrooms, sliced

½ cup baby corn

1½ tablespoons gluten-free cornflour (cornstarch)

2 tablespoons gluten-free soy sauce

2 tablespoons fermented black beans, crushed

½ cup water

Cook the rice as per packet instructions. Cover and keep warm.

Meanwhile, heat the sesame oil in a wok over medium heat. Add the garlic, ginger, chilli and beef strips and stir-fry for 4–5 minutes or until browned. Remove from the pan. Increase the heat to medium–high, add the bok choy, snow peas, mushrooms and baby corn and stir-fry for 2–3 minutes or until tender.

In a small bowl, combine the cornflour with the soy sauce, crushed black beans and a little of the water to form a paste. Gradually add the remaining water and stir until well blended. Return the beef strips to the pan and pour the black bean mixture over the beef and vegetables. Heat through, stirring, until the sauce has thickened. Serve with the rice.

Tuna, Tomato and Olive Pasta

Gluten-free pasta is now readily available in supermarkets, in all sorts of shapes and varieties.
If you can't find spirals, spaghetti or fettuccine would work just as well.

Serves 4

250 g (9 oz) gluten-free spiral pasta

⅓ cup olive oil

1 clove garlic, finely sliced

2 rashers bacon, finely chopped

½ cup pitted black olives

1 fresh red chilli, seeded and finely sliced

425 g (15 oz) tin tuna, drained

2 tomatoes, diced

1 cup grated parmesan

2 tablespoons chopped parsley

salt

freshly ground black pepper

Bring a large saucepan of water to the boil and cook the pasta as per packet instructions. When al dente, drain and return to the pan. Toss a little olive oil through the cooked pasta and cover to keep warm.

Heat 2 tablespoons olive oil in a large frying pan over medium heat, add the garlic, bacon, olives and chilli, and cook for 1–2 minutes. Add the tuna, tomato and remaining olive oil, and cook until the tomatoes are soft. Increase the heat and stir in the cooked pasta, parmesan and parsley. Leave in the pan without stirring to make the bacon crispy, but don't let it burn. Season to taste and serve.

Herbed Fish

Herbed Fish

Fresh herbs. Fresh fish. These are the essential ingredients for this simple dish. Snapper and barramundi are ideal. Serve with steamed rice, lime wedges and sprigs of coriander (cilantro).

Serves 4

1 cup chopped mixed herbs (eg rosemary, parsley, oregano, thyme)

½ teaspoon salt

¼ teaspoon coarsely ground black pepper

4 × 150 g (5½ oz) firm white fish fillets

3–4 tablespoons olive oil

2 cloves garlic, crushed

Combine the herbs, salt and pepper in a shallow bowl. Brush each fish fillet with olive oil, then press into the herbs, ensuring the fillets are well coated on both sides.

Heat 2 tablespoons olive oil in a large non-stick frying pan over medium–high heat. Add the garlic and cook for 1–2 minutes or until golden brown. Add the fish fillets and cook for 2 minutes each side or until just cooked through.

Pasta with Smoked Chicken and Bacon

Anyone who knows me knows that smoked chicken is one of my favourite foods, and here it is in my all-time favourite pasta dish.

Serves 4

500 g (1 lb 2 oz) gluten-free pasta

5 tablespoons olive oil

2 cloves garlic, crushed

200 g (7 oz) smoked chicken breast, sliced

200 g (7 oz) bacon, cut into small strips

⅓ cup chopped thyme

½ cup grated parmesan

salt

freshly ground black pepper

Bring a large saucepan of water to the boil and cook the pasta as per packet instructions. When al dente, drain and return to the pan. Toss 2 tablespoons olive oil through the cooked pasta and cover to keep warm.

Heat 1 tablespoon olive oil in a large frying pan over medium heat, add the garlic, smoked chicken and bacon and cook until the bacon is golden brown. Stir in the warm pasta, thyme, parmesan and 2 tablespoons olive oil, and toss gently until the parmesan has melted. Season with salt and pepper to taste, and drizzle with a little more olive oil, if desired.

Rib Eye Steaks with Mushroom Sauce and Pea Mash

With its vibrant and inviting colours, this dish presents really nicely. It's perfect washed down with a glass of gluten-free beer.

Serves 6

1 tablespoon olive oil

1 tablespoon lemon juice

2 cloves garlic, crushed

salt

freshly ground black pepper

6 x 200 g (7 oz) rib-eye steaks

PEA MASH

500 g (1 lb 2 oz) baby peas

20 g (¾ oz) butter

MUSHROOM SAUCE

30 g (1 oz) butter

500 g (1 lb 2 oz) button mushrooms, sliced

½ cup gluten-free beef stock

3 tablespoons chopped parsley

½ cup reduced-fat cream

Combine the olive oil, lemon juice, garlic, and some salt and pepper in a large bowl. Add the steaks and toss gently to coat. Cover with plastic film and marinate in the refrigerator for at least 3 hours.

Preheat a grill plate, chargrill pan or barbecue to medium–high and cook the steaks to your liking. Cover and leave to rest while you make the mash and sauce.

To make the mash, cook the peas in a medium saucepan of boiling water for 5 minutes or until tender. Drain and place in a medium bowl; add the butter, season with salt and pepper and mash together. Cover and keep warm.

To make the sauce, melt the butter in a small frying pan over medium–low heat, add the mushrooms and cook gently for 5 minutes or until soft. Add the beef stock, parsley and cream, season with salt and pepper and simmer until the sauce thickens slightly.

Spoon the mash onto warmed plates, top with the steaks and finish with the mushroom sauce.

❖ *If you are lactose intolerant, only a small serve of the sauce is recommended.*

Vegetarian Dinners

Lemon, Garlic and Oregano Polenta with Dressed Spinach

To me, polenta is an unsung hero. It is versatile, inexpensive and satisfying, yet many people still have not experienced the pleasure of cooking with it. In this dish, the polenta is firm and has wonderful fresh flavours.

Serves 6

3 cups gluten-free vegetable stock

1 cup polenta

3 cloves garlic, crushed

1 tablespoon finely grated lemon zest

2 tablespoons chopped oregano

200 g (7 oz) goat's cheese, crumbled

3 tablespoons olive oil

DRESSED SPINACH

3 tablespoons olive oil

1–2 tablespoons balsamic vinegar

4 cups baby spinach leaves

Grease a 20 cm (8 inch) square baking dish.

Place the vegetable stock in a medium saucepan and bring to the boil over medium–high heat. Add the polenta, garlic and lemon zest, reduce the heat and simmer for 15 minutes or until the mixture is thick and firm to stir. Remove from the heat, allow to cool for 5 minutes, then stir in the oregano and goat's cheese.

Pour the mixture into the baking dish and smooth the surface. Set aside to cool to room temperature, then cover with plastic film and place in the refrigerator for 3 hours.

When firm, cut the polenta into six pieces. Brush each side with olive oil and cook under a hot grill or in a chargrill pan for 2–3 minutes each side, or until nicely browned and warmed through.

To make the dressed spinach, mix together the olive oil and balsamic vinegar. Drizzle over the spinach leaves and toss gently. Serve with the warm polenta.

Sweet and Spicy Tofu

*Bold flavours are created from the combination of herbs and spices in this recipe,
which in turn makes the tofu come alive. Serve with steamed rice.*

Serves 4

2 tablespoons canola oil

⅓ cup gluten-free soy sauce

⅓ cup Chinese rice wine

3 teaspoons finely chopped ginger

2 whole star anise

1 teaspoon Chinese five-spice powder

1 teaspoon allspice

1 tablespoon gluten-free cornflour (cornstarch)

2 tablespoons brown sugar

large strip of orange zest

750 g (1 lb 10 oz) firm tofu, cut into 1.5 cm (½ inch) cubes

200 g (7 oz) snow peas (mange-tout), topped and tailed

1 cinnamon stick

1 cup water

3 tablespoons chopped coriander (cilantro) leaves

Combine the canola oil, soy sauce, rice wine, spices, cornflour, brown sugar and orange zest
in a large bowl. Add the tofu, toss gently to coat, then cover and refrigerate for 3–4 hours
or overnight.

Heat a large frying pan over medium–low heat, add the tofu, with its marinade, snow peas,
cinnamon stick and water. Cook, stirring continuously, until the snow peas have softened.
Remove the star anise, cinnamon stick and orange zest, and stir in the coriander.

Pumpkin and Ricotta Buckwheat Crepes

I was inspired to make this dish after a beautiful meal at a winery in the Yarra Valley. I hope you, too, can enjoy it in the company of good friends and good wine.

Serves 4

CREPES

500 g (1 lb 2 oz) pumpkin, cut into large chunks

¾ cup rice flour

½ cup gluten-free cornflour (cornstarch)

⅓ cup buckwheat flour

¾ teaspoon bicarbonate of soda

2 eggs, lightly beaten

1½ cups reduced-fat milk

40 g (1½ oz) butter, melted

250 g (9 oz) reduced-fat ricotta

2 eggs, extra

salt

freshly ground black pepper

SAUCE

2 tablespoons gluten-free cornflour (cornstarch)

1 cup reduced-fat cream

1 cup pureed tomato (passata)

1 cup grated reduced-fat cheddar

Preheat the oven to 180°C (350°F). Grease a 30 cm (12 inch) × 18 cm (7 inch) baking dish. Boil the pumpkin until tender, then drain and cool to room temperature. Puree with a hand blender until smooth, then set aside to cool completely.

Sift the flours and bicarbonate of soda into a medium bowl three times (or mix well with a whisk to ensure they are well combined). Add the egg and milk and mix with a spoon to form a smooth batter. Stir in the melted butter. Cover and leave to rest for 20 minutes.

Heat a large heavy-based frying pan over medium heat and spray with non-stick spray. Pour the batter into the pan and cook until bubbles appear, then turn and cook the other side. Repeat with the remaining batter to make eight crepes. Keep warm in the oven.

To make the sauce, place the cornflour in a small bowl and blend with ¼ cup cream to form a paste. Add the pureed tomato and remaining cream and stir until well combined. Pour into a small saucepan over medium heat and stir until thickened (do not boil). Add the grated cheddar and stir until melted. Season to taste with salt and pepper.

To make the filling for the crepes, combine the pumpkin, ricotta, extra eggs, salt and pepper. Place spoonfuls of the filling in a line along the centre of each crepe. Roll up and place in the baking dish. Pour the sauce over the top and bake for 30 minutes.

◇ *This recipe is unsuitable for people with lactose intolerance.*

Gnocchi with Blue Cheese Sauce

Don't let the thought of making gnocchi overwhelm you – the trick is to make sure you don't cook too many at once. Chopped herbs can be added to the base recipe for a fresh variation. If you are not cooking the gnocchi immediately, sprinkle lightly with flour, cover with a clean tea towel and set aside at room temperature for up to 2 hours.

Serves 4

800 g (1 lb 12 oz) small desiree potatoes

1 teaspoon salt

freshly ground black pepper

⅓ cup potato flour

⅓ cup fine rice flour

BLUE CHEESE SAUCE

1¼ cups reduced-fat cream

3 cloves garlic, crushed

150 g (5½ oz) blue cheese

Peel the potatoes and place in a large saucepan of boiling water. Cook whole for 10–12 minutes or until soft (easily pierced with a skewer). Drain and set aside for 10 minutes to cool slightly. Place the warm potatoes in a large bowl, add the salt and season to taste with pepper. Mash with a potato masher until the mixture is very smooth.

Mix the flours together in a medium bowl, then add to the mashed potato. Use your hand to make a stiff, slightly sticky dough that leaves the side of the bowl. Take care not to overwork the dough as it will become too sticky.

Cut the dough into four even portions. Roll one portion into a long sausage about 2 cm (¾ inch) thick on a lightly floured surface. Using a knife dusted in flour, cut the dough into 2 cm (¾ inch) pieces. Place on a flat baking tray lined with a floured tea towel, spacing the gnocchi so the pieces don't touch. Repeat with remaining portions of dough.

Bring a large saucepan of water to the boil. Add the gnocchi in batches (they should sit in a single layer on the base of the pan) – they may stick together if overcrowded. Remove with a slotted spoon when they all rise to the surface. Drain, and transfer to warmed plates. Cover loosely with foil.

To make the sauce, heat the cream and garlic in a small frying pan over medium–high heat for 2–3 minutes or until just about boiling. Reduce the heat to low and add the blue cheese. Stir for 2–3 minutes or until the cheese has melted and the sauce is smooth. Season with salt and pepper, then pour over the gnocchi.

◇ *This recipe is unsuitable for people with lactose intolerance.*

Marinated Capsicum Risotto

The tri-colours of the capsicums in this dish make it a visual delight – and your tastebuds won't be disappointed either.

Serves 4

1 large red capsicum (pepper)

1 large green capsicum (pepper)

1 large yellow capsicum (pepper)

2 teaspoons olive oil

2 tablespoons red wine vinegar

3 tablespoons olive oil, extra

3 tablespoons chopped parsley

2 cloves garlic, crushed

salt

freshly ground black pepper

8 cups gluten-free vegetable stock

2½ cups arborio rice

½ cup dry white wine

½ cup reduced-fat cream

½ cup grated parmesan

3 tablespoons chopped parsley, extra

Preheat the grill to medium–high. Cut each capsicum into quarters and remove the seeds. Arrange the pieces, skin-side up, on a flat baking tray and drizzle with olive oil. Cook under the grill for 8–10 minutes or until the flesh is tender and the skin is charred. Cover with foil and set aside for about 10 minutes. Peel off the skin and cut the flesh into 5 mm (¼ inch) wide strips.

Combine the capsicum strips with the red wine vinegar, extra olive oil, parsley, garlic, salt and pepper. Cover and marinate in the refrigerator for 1–2 hours.

Heat the vegetable stock in a medium saucepan, then cover and keep at a gentle simmer over low heat.

Put the rice in a large saucepan over medium heat, stir in the wine and cook until absorbed. Add 1 cup of the hot stock and stir until it is completely absorbed. Repeat this process, adding ½ cup of stock at a time until all but the last ½ cup of stock has been added. Stir in the marinated capsicum pieces, then add the remaining stock, stirring until completely absorbed. Add the cream, parmesan and extra parsley, season with salt and pepper and mix together well. Serve immediately.

Curried Vegetable Patties

These patties are terrific as the feature in a main meal, with a salad on the side, but make sure you save any leftovers – they make a quick and tasty lunch on the run.

Serves 4

3 large potatoes, cut into quarters

450 g (1 lb) firm tofu, finely chopped

1 stalk celery, very finely sliced

½ red capsicum (pepper), seeded and diced

3 tablespoons tinned corn kernels

2 eggs

1 tablespoon toasted cumin seeds

4 tablespoons gluten-free curry powder
(adjust according to your liking)

½ cup gluten-free breadcrumbs

salt

freshly ground black pepper

½ cup gluten-free breadcrumbs, extra

vegetable oil, for pan-frying

Boil the potatoes until soft. Drain, then place in a medium bowl and mash with a potato masher until smooth. Allow to cool slightly.

Combine the mashed potato, tofu, celery, capsicum, corn, eggs, cumin seeds, curry powder, breadcrumbs, salt and pepper in a large bowl. Cover and refrigerate for 1 hour.

Pour the extra breadcrumbs into a shallow bowl. Shape the potato mixture into eight round patties, then coat the patties in the breadcrumbs.

Heat a little oil in a non-stick frying pan over medium–low heat. Add the patties and cook for 5–6 minutes each side or until golden and cooked through.

Sweet Potato, Sweet Corn and Goat's Cheese Frittata

I've always considered frittata to be an excellent dish to explore so many flavours. This one is satisfying, inexpensive and dairy-free. Serve with a salad drizzled with olive oil and balsamic vinegar.

Serves 4–6

400 g (14 oz) sweet potato, cut into 5 cm (2 inch) chunks

6 eggs, lightly beaten

420 g (15 oz) tin gluten-free creamed corn

2 cloves garlic, crushed

salt

freshly ground black pepper

100 g (3½ oz) goat's cheese, crumbled

salad leaves, to serve

olive oil, to serve

balsamic vinegar, to serve

Preheat the oven to 180°C (350°F). Grease a 16 cm (6¼ inch) square baking dish.

Boil the sweet potato over medium heat for about 10 minutes or until just tender – do not overcook. Drain. Allow to cool, then slice thinly.

Place the egg, creamed corn, garlic, salt and pepper in a large bowl and mix together well.

Combine the sweet potato and goat's cheese in the baking dish, then pour the egg mixture over the top. Tilt the baking dish to ensure the egg mixture is evenly distributed and fills all the gaps. Bake for 25–30 minutes or until golden brown. Leave for 5 minutes before serving (you can also serve this cold or at room temperature).

Sweet Potato, Sweet Corn
and Goat's Cheese Frittata

Tofu and Sesame Stir-fry

If you can't find vermicelli noodles, rice or mung bean (glass) noodles can be used instead. Buy them from Asian grocery stores.

Serves 4

1 clove garlic, crushed

1 teaspoon grated ginger

3 tablespoons gluten-free soy sauce

3 tablespoons sushi vinegar

1 tablespoon sesame oil

200 g (7 oz) puffed tofu squares

250 g (9 oz) vermicelli noodles

200 g (7 oz) snow peas (mange-tout), topped and tailed

400 g (14 oz) broccoli, cut into small florets

1 teaspoon Dijon mustard

1 tablespoon brown sugar

2 tablespoons sesame oil, extra

2 tablespoons sesame seeds, toasted

Combine the garlic, ginger, soy sauce, sushi vinegar and sesame oil in a large bowl. Add the tofu and toss gently to coat. Cover and refrigerate for 2 hours.

Soak the noodles in a large bowl of hot water for 4–5 minutes or until softened. Drain, rinse under cold water, drain again and set aside.

Drain the tofu, reserving the marinade. Heat a large frying pan over medium heat, add the tofu and cook, stirring gently, for 2–3 minutes. Add the snow peas and broccoli, and cook for 3–5 minutes or until tender.

Combine the mustard, brown sugar, extra sesame oil and reserved marinade in a small bowl. Pour over the tofu and vegetables and stir to combine. Add the noodles and toasted sesame seeds to the pan and toss gently until warmed through.

Pesto Pizza

Pesto Pizza

Pesto is one of my favourite flavour bases, and who doesn't love pizza? The combination of the two makes this recipe an absolute winner.

Makes 6 small pizzas

2 cups gluten-free bread mix

2 teaspoons olive oil

3 tablespoons prepared gluten-free pesto

1 cup grated mozzarella

3 ripe tomatoes, sliced

200 g (7 oz) bocconcini, cut into slices

basil leaves, to garnish

Preheat the oven to 120°C (250°F). Line two or three baking trays with baking paper.

Prepare the bread mix following the directions on the packet. Spoon ⅓ cup of the bread dough onto one of the baking trays and, using the back of a metal spoon, spread out the dough to form a 15 cm (6 inch) round about 5 mm (¼ inch) thick. Dip the spoon in water to prevent sticking if required. Repeat with the remaining bread dough to form six bases. Drizzle a little olive oil over each base and spread evenly with the back of a spoon. Bake for 15 minutes or until lightly browned. Remove from the oven, and increase the temperature to 180°C (350°F).

Spread the pesto over the pizza bases and top with grated mozzarella. Layer with alternate slices of tomato and bocconcini. Bake for 15 minutes or until the cheese has melted (place directly on the wire rack of the oven if you prefer a crispy base). Garnish with basil leaves and serve immediately.

Asian Mushroom Omelette

There really is no substitute for the oyster and enoki mushrooms in this recipe. They are full of flavour and work brilliantly for this Asian dish.

Serves 4

1 tablespoon sesame oil

1 clove garlic, crushed

200 g (7 oz) oyster mushrooms, sliced

100 g (3½ oz) enoki mushrooms

1 cup chopped Chinese cabbage

8 eggs

3 tablespoons gluten-free oyster sauce

salt

freshly ground black pepper

Preheat the oven to 150°C (300°F).

Heat the sesame oil in a small frying pan over medium heat. Add the garlic, mushrooms and cabbage, and cook for 5–8 minutes or until softened. Remove from the heat.

Whisk the eggs in a medium bowl, add the mushroom mixture, oyster sauce, salt and pepper, and mix together well. Pour a quarter of the mixture into a small frying pan and cook until almost set on top. Carefully lift the edges with a spatula, and shake the omelette loose. Place the pan under a hot grill until the top of the omelette is set.

Fold the omelette in half and keep warm in the oven while cooking the remaining omelettes. Alternatively, cook all the eggs together in a large frying pan and cut the omelette into quarters before serving.

Middle Eastern Rice

I always feel the brown rice in this dish gives a sense of good soul food, enhanced by the characteristic flavours of the Middle East. As a variation, whole millet grains can be used instead of the rice.

Serves 4

500 g (1 lb 2 oz) pumpkin, cut into 2 cm (¾ inch) pieces

3 tablespoons olive oil

salt

freshly ground black pepper

4 cups gluten-free vegetable stock

1½ cups brown rice, rinsed

1 clove garlic, crushed

2 teaspoons cumin seeds

1 teaspoon powdered saffron

1 large eggplant (aubergine), cut into 2 cm (¾ inch) cubes

½ cup salted cashews, toasted

1–2 tablespoons lemon juice

1 cup chopped coriander (cilantro) leaves

Preheat the oven to 180°C (350°F).

Place the pumpkin pieces on a baking tray, drizzle with 1 tablespoon of the olive oil and season with salt and pepper. Roast for 30 minutes or until golden brown. Set aside to cool.

Place the vegetable stock in a small saucepan and bring to the boil over medium–high heat. Add the rice, reduce the heat to low and simmer, covered, for 45 minutes or until the stock is absorbed and the rice is tender. Add a little more stock if required. Rinse and drain, then set aside to cool to room temperature.

Heat the remaining olive oil in a medium frying pan, add the garlic, cumin and saffron and cook for 1–2 minutes or until fragrant. Add the eggplant and cashews and cook for 5–10 minutes or until the eggplant has softened and cashews have browned. Remove from the heat, and leave to cool to room temperature.

Put the cooled pumpkin, rice, eggplant, cashews, lemon juice and chopped coriander in a large bowl and gently toss together. Season to taste with salt and pepper.

Healthy Side Dishes

Fresh seasonal vegetables brimming with flavour and texture add so much to a meal.

Gluten-free does not mean taste-free. Everyone will enjoy these great gluten-free sides, which are as flavoursome as they are healthy.

Fresh seasonal vegetables brimming with flavour and texture add so much to a meal and we are lucky to have such a variety at our fingertips. Simply prepared with a drizzle of olive oil or a sprinkling of fresh herbs, they make a statement of their own. Of course you can take it further, add a few more ingredients and create a flavoursome foil for the main course. For those of us on a gluten-free diet, these side dishes fulfill the role that is often taken by the bread basket.

The ideas and recipes that follow take their inspiration from a variety of cuisines, and I have also ensured they are largely dairy- or lactose-free to cater for those who have multiple food intolerances or have other reasons for food restrictions. I've chosen ingredients that are easy to buy, allowing you to make and enjoy the recipes with minimal fuss.

Adding a spoonful of this or a handful of that can transform a bowl of crisp salad greens or steamed vegetables. I've listed some great-tasting flavourings on the facing page.

Dressing up your greens

- Balsamic vinegar

- Gluten-free dukkah (a Middle Eastern blend of spices and nuts)

- Tapenade (olive, anchovy)

- Salsa (onion-free options for IBS)

- Flavoured butters (herb, garlic, wasabi, anchovy, olive)

- Kasundi (Indian chutney; onion-free for IBS)

- Mirin

- Lime and/or lemon juice

- Chopped fresh herbs

- Flavoured mayonnaise (caper and dill, lemon)

- Toasted nuts (pine nuts, walnuts, almonds)

- Toasted seeds (pumpkin, sesame, sunflower)

- Shavings of cheese (parmesan, pecorino, ricotta, blue cheese, fetta)

- Crispy pan-fried bacon

Healthy Sides

- **Ginger and Sesame Asian Greens:** Chop 4 cups of your favourite Asian greens (eg bok choy (pak choi), choi sum or gai laan) into even-sized pieces, about 3 cm (1¼ inches) long. Bring a large saucepan of water to the boil, add the greens and gently blanch for 1–2 minutes, then remove the pan from the heat. Place a wok over medium–high heat. When hot, add 3 tablespoons sesame oil and swirl to coat. Add 1 crushed clove garlic, 1 tablespoon grated ginger, 1 tablespoon sesame seeds and the blanched vegetables. Toss until heated through and well combined. *Serves 4–6*

- **Mediterranean Potato Salad:** Place 16 small potatoes in a large saucepan of cold water. Cover and bring to the boil over high heat, then boil for 8–10 minutes or until tender. Drain and set aside to cool. Heat 2 teaspoons olive oil in a medium frying pan over medium heat, add 1 cup sliced mushrooms and cook for 3–5 minutes or until softened. Season with salt and freshly ground black pepper. Remove from the heat and leave to cool to room temperature. Place 3 tablespoons whole-egg gluten-free mayonnaise, ½ cup prepared basil pesto and 3 tablespoons chopped parsley in a small bowl and mix together well. Cut the potatoes in half and place in a large bowl. Add the mushrooms, 1 cup chopped pitted black olives and the mayonnaise dressing, and toss gently to combine. *Serves 6–8*

- **Brown Rice Salad:** Heat 1 tablespoon peanut oil in a large frying pan over medium heat, add 2 crushed cloves of garlic, 3 tablespoons unsalted peanuts and 2 cups baby spinach leaves and heat until the spinach has wilted and the peanuts are golden brown. Add 4 cups cooked brown rice to the pan and stir until well combined. Remove from the heat and leave to cool to room temperature. Place 1 tablespoon peanut oil and 3 tablespoons whole-egg gluten-free mayonnaise in a small bowl and mix together well. Place the rice mixture, ½ cup sliced sundried tomatoes, 2 stalks celery, sliced, ½ cup sultanas and ½ cup chopped parsley in a large bowl. Add the dressing and toss gently to combine. *Serves 6–8*

- **Ratatouille:** Cut 3 large zucchini (courgettes) in half lengthways, then thinly slice. Cut 1 large red capsicum (pepper) and 2 medium eggplant (aubergines) into long strips. Heat 1 tablespoon olive oil in a large frying pan over medium heat, add 2 crushed cloves garlic and ½ teaspoon chilli powder and cook for 1–2 minutes. Add the zucchini, capsicum and eggplant, and cook, stirring regularly, until the vegetables have softened. Stir in a 410 g (14½ oz) tin of tomatoes, reduce the heat to medium–low and cook, stirring occasionally, for 15 minutes or until the mixture thickens. Remove from the heat, stir in 2 tablespoons chopped parsley and season with salt and freshly ground black pepper. *Serves 4*

Desserts

Self-saucing Chocolate Pudding

Having been diagnosed with coeliac disease as an adult, I adapted the recipe I was served as a child to ensure I can still devour delicious chocolate pudding!

85 g (3 oz) fine rice flour

3 tablespoons gluten-free cornflour (cornstarch)

3 tablespoons soy flour

1 teaspoon bicarbonate of soda

2 teaspoons gluten-free baking powder

1 teaspoon xanthan gum (optional)

140 g (5 oz) castor (superfine) sugar

½ cup cocoa powder

¾ cup low-fat milk

1 teaspoon vanilla essence

2 eggs, lightly beaten

40 g (1½ oz) unsalted butter, melted

150 g (5½ oz) brown sugar

2 tablespoons cocoa powder, extra

1¾ cups hot water

whipped cream, to serve

Preheat the oven to 180°C (350°F). Grease a 6-cup baking dish.

Sift the flours, bicarbonate of soda, baking powder, xanthan gum, castor sugar and cocoa powder three times into a medium bowl (or mix well with a whisk to ensure they are well combined).

In a separate bowl, combine the milk, vanilla essence, egg and butter. Add to the dry ingredients and stir until well combined. Pour the mixture into the baking dish.

Combine the brown sugar, extra cocoa powder and hot water, and pour over the pudding. Bake for 45–55 minutes or until the pudding has a crisp, spongy top and rich fudge sauce base. Serve with cream.

◇ *The milk can be replaced with lactose-free milk.*

Crème Caramel with Hazelnut Liqueur

This version has a twist on the traditional recipe with a subtle addition of hazelnut liqueur in both the sauce and the custard. Coffee liqueur also works brilliantly.

Serves 4

SAUCE
¾ cup castor (superfine) sugar
5 tablespoons water
1½ tablespoons hazelnut liqueur

CUSTARD
2 cups milk
4 eggs
1 egg yolk
½ cup castor (superfine) sugar
2½ tablespoons hazelnut liqueur
(more if you like)

Preheat the oven to 140°C (275°F). Grease four ¾-cup ramekin dishes.

To make the sauce, place the castor sugar and water in a small saucepan over medium heat and cook, stirring regularly, for 10–15 minutes or until lightly browned and caramelised. Remove from the heat and stir in the hazelnut liqueur.

To make the custard, bring the milk to the boil in a medium saucepan. Set aside to cool slightly. Whisk the eggs, egg yolk and castor sugar together in a medium bowl, then whisk in the milk and hazelnut liqueur.

Place the ramekin dishes in a deep baking dish. Divide the sauce among the dishes, then pour the custard over the sauce to fill each ramekin. Pour enough water into the baking dish to come halfway up the sides of the ramekins. Bake for 40 minutes or until just set. Remove from the oven and leave to cool, then refrigerate for 3 hours or until set.

Turn out onto dessert plates and serve.

◇ *The milk can be replaced with lactose-free milk.*

Sticky Rice

Although the recipe calls for glutinous rice there is NO gluten in any rice! It refers to the sticky texture the rice develops as it cooks. Glutinous rice can be found in Asian grocery stores. This dessert has a fantastic burst of flavour you will just love.

Serves 4

1 cup glutinous rice

2 teaspoons coconut essence

1 cup low-fat milk

¾ cup water

½ cup castor (superfine) sugar

finely grated zest of 1 lemon

1 stalk lemongrass, bruised

¼ teaspoon vanilla essence

2 tablespoons reduced-fat cream

Soak the rice in a bowl of cold water for 6 hours. Drain, rinse and drain again.

Place the rice in a medium saucepan and add the coconut essence, milk, water, castor sugar and lemon zest. Place the lemongrass over the rice and cook over medium–high heat for 40 minutes or until the rice is tender and fragrant. Remove the lemongrass stalk, and stir in the vanilla essence and cream just before serving.

◇ *The milk can be replaced with lactose-free milk.*

Classic Pavlova with Berry Coulis

Lining the tin with baking paper is very important to the success of this recipe – it helps the pavlova keep its structure as the shell sets, ensuring a perfect result every time.

Serves 10–12

5 egg whites, at room temperature

1 cup castor (superfine) sugar

2 teaspoons gluten-free cornflour (cornstarch)

1 teaspoon vanilla essence

1 teaspoon lemon juice

1¼ cups thickened cream, whipped

fruit (eg pulp of 4 large passionfruit, sliced banana or fresh berries), to serve

BERRY COULIS

200 g (7 oz) fresh raspberries

150 g (5½ oz) fresh blueberries

1½ tablespoons pure icing (confectioner's) sugar, sifted

½ teaspoon vanilla essence

Preheat the oven to 100°C (200°F).

Line the base of a 19 cm (7½ inch) springform tin with baking paper. Also line the edges, with the paper extending up well above the height of the tin. Use a metal paperclip to fasten the paper. Place the springform tin on a flat baking tray.

Using electric beaters, beat the egg whites in a large clean bowl until firm peaks form. Gradually add the sugar, 2 tablespoons at a time, beating well between additions, until the mixture is thick and glossy. Add the cornflour, vanilla essence and lemon juice, and beat until well combined.

Spoon the mixture into the tin and carefully smooth the surface. Bake for 1–1¼ hours or until the meringue is crisp on the outside. Leave the oven door ajar and allow the pavlova to cool for 2 hours. Close the oven door and allow the pavlova to cool for a further 4–5 hours or overnight.

To make the berry coulis, place the raspberries, blueberries, icing sugar and vanilla essence in a blender or the bowl of a food processor. Blend until smooth. Pour into an airtight container, seal and chill in the refrigerator for at least 1 hour.

Spread the whipped cream over the cold pavlova, then arrange the fruit over the top. Serve with the berry coulis.

Blueberry and Rhubarb Crumble

Tinned blueberries actually work better than fresh berries in this recipe, as their pre-softened texture blends particularly well with the rhubarb, giving a lovely consistent flavour.

Serves 8

700 g (1 lb 9 oz) rhubarb, stalks cut into 3 cm (1¼ inch) pieces

½ cup sugar

2 x 425 g (15 oz) tins blueberries in syrup, drained

3 tablespoons pure icing (confectioner's) sugar

¾ cup fine rice flour

½ cup brown sugar

2 tablespoons desiccated coconut

60 g (2¼ oz) butter, at room temperature, cubed

vanilla ice cream, to serve

Preheat the oven to 180°C (350°F). Grease a 20 cm (8 inch) square baking dish.

Combine the rhubarb and sugar in a large saucepan of boiling water and cook for about 10 minutes or until tender. Cool in the liquid for 10 minutes (this helps retain the rich red colour). Drain.

Place the cooked rhubarb, blueberries and icing sugar in a medium bowl and stir until well combined. Spoon the mixture into the baking dish.

Combine the rice flour, brown sugar and desiccated coconut in a small bowl. Rub in the butter until the mixture resembles fine breadcrumbs. Sprinkle evenly over the fruit and bake for 30 minutes or until golden brown. Serve with ice cream.

Rum and Raisin Baked Ricotta

Make sure you buy good-quality fresh ricotta as it is the signature ingredient in this dish. Enhanced with rum-soaked raisins, each mouthful has a subtle but exciting flavour.

Serves 8

⅓ cup raisins

2 tablespoons rum

2½ tablespoons sugar

750 g (1 lb 10 oz) fresh ricotta

3 eggs

1 teaspoon vanilla essence

chocolate ice cream, to serve

CHOCOLATE RUM SAUCE

50 g (1¾ oz) butter

½ cup firmly packed brown sugar

½ cup reduced-fat cream

2 tablespoons cocoa powder

50 g (1¾ oz) dark chocolate buttons

1–2 tablespoons rum

Combine the raisins and rum in a small bowl and leave to soak for at least 3 hours, preferably overnight.

Preheat the oven to 160°C (315°F). Lightly grease eight ½-cup ramekin dishes or metal dariole moulds.

Combine the sugar, ricotta, eggs and vanilla essence in a medium bowl and blend with a metal spoon or electric beaters until well combined. Alternatively, blend the mixture in a food processor for a really smooth texture. Add the soaked raisins and stir only enough to ensure the raisins are evenly distributed through the ricotta.

Pour the mixture into the ramekin dishes. Place the dishes in a large baking dish and pour in enough boiling water to come halfway up the sides of the ramekins. Cover the whole baking dish with foil and bake for 30 minutes. Remove the ramekins from the baking dish and leave to cool to room temperature on the bench. Invert the ramekins onto plates and place in the refrigerator to cool completely before serving.

To make the chocolate rum sauce, melt the butter in a small saucepan over low heat. Add the brown sugar, cream, cocoa powder and chocolate buttons, and stir until the chocolate has melted and the sauce is smooth. Stir in the rum.

Serve the baked ricotta with chocolate ice cream and chocolate rum sauce.

◇ *This recipe is unsuitable for people with lactose intolerance.*

Sticky Date Pudding

I know I am a dietitian and this is probably a naughty confession to make, but I do consider dessert to be the best part of a meal, and this sticky date pudding is one of my absolute favourites. If you are a fructose malabsorber, reduce the quantity of dates to ⅔ cup.

Serves 10

1½ cups pitted dates

½ cup boiling water

100 g (3½ oz) butter, at room temperature

165 g (5¾ oz) castor (superfine) sugar

1 teaspoon vanilla essence

2 eggs

50 g (1¾ oz) gluten-free cornflour (cornstarch)

130 g (4½ oz) fine rice flour

50 g (1¾ oz) soy flour

1 teaspoon bicarbonate of soda

2 teaspoons gluten-free baking powder

2 tablespoons ground ginger

1 teaspoon xanthan gum (optional)

CARAMEL SAUCE

110 g (3¾ oz) brown sugar

40 g (1½ oz) butter

½ cup reduced-fat cream

Grease a 20 cm (8 inch) pudding basin and line the base with baking paper.

Put the dates in a small bowl and soak in the boiling water for 15–20 minutes. Set aside to cool to room temperature.

Place the butter, sugar and vanilla essence in a medium bowl and beat with electric beaters until well combined. Add the eggs, one at a time, beating well between additions. Stir in the dates.

Sift the flours, bicarbonate of soda, baking powder, ginger and xanthan gum three times into a medium bowl (or mix well with a whisk to ensure they are well combined). Add to the egg mixture and stir with a wooden spoon to gently combine. Spoon the mixture into the pudding basin and smooth the surface.

Place the pudding basin in a large stockpot. Fill the stockpot with enough boiling water to come halfway up the side of the basin. Cook over medium–low heat for 60–65 minutes or until the pudding is cooked. Check by inserting a skewer – if it comes out clean the pudding is ready.

To make the caramel sauce, combine the brown sugar, butter and cream in a small saucepan. Stir constantly over medium–low heat for 8–10 minutes or until the sugar has dissolved and the sauce has thickened. Spoon over the pudding.

Passionfruit Mousse

This light and fluffy mousse is a real treat. If you are using fresh passionfruit pulp rather than tinned pulp in syrup, you'll need to increase the sugar by about half a cup.

Serves 6

½ cup boiling water

1½ tablespoons powdered gelatine

4 large eggs, at room temperature, separated

1⅓ cups tinned passionfruit pulp

1¼ cups thickened cream

¾ cup castor (superfine) sugar

Set aside a large bowl filled with two trays of ice cubes.

Combine the boiling water and gelatine in a small heatproof bowl. Sit the bowl over a larger bowl of boiling water, stirring constantly until the gelatine has completely dissolved. Leave to cool to room temperature.

Place the egg yolks in a medium bowl and beat with electric beaters until thick and creamy and tripled in size. Fold in the passionfruit pulp and cooled gelatine.

Pour the cream into a large bowl and beat with electric beaters until thick.

Clean the beaters thoroughly, then place the egg whites in a clean medium bowl and beat with electric beaters until soft peaks form. Add the sugar, 3 tablespoons at a time, and beat until well dissolved.

Using a large metal spoon, fold the passionfruit mixture into the thickened cream, then gently fold in the egg-white mixture until well combined. Spoon into individual bowls and refrigerate until set.

◇ *This recipe is unsuitable for people with lactose intolerance.*

Warm Lemon Sago

Sago has made a comeback! This modern take on an old favourite is served warm and brings together a wonderfully creamy texture and a delicious tart lemon flavour.

Serves 6

4 lemons

4 cups low-fat milk

⅓ cup sago

⅓ cup castor (superfine) sugar

Using a vegetable peeler, cut slices of lemon zest into 2 cm (¾ inch) strips. Squeeze the lemons to give ½ cup of juice.

Place the milk and lemon zest in a medium saucepan and gradually bring to a simmer over high heat. Reduce the heat to low and simmer for 2 minutes. Discard the pieces of lemon zest.

Add the sago to the milk, stirring well to combine. Simmer over low heat, stirring regularly, for 20–25 minutes or until the sago resembles translucent jelly-like balls.

Remove from the heat. Stir in the castor sugar and lemon juice, then pour into six glass bowls. Serve immediately.

◇ *The milk can be replaced with lactose-free milk.*

Rhubarb Cream Pie

The key to success with the pastry is ice-cold water, but not too much (use even less in warm weather). The star of the show is the soft smooth texture of the rhubarb filling.

Serves 8–10

PASTRY
130 g (4½ oz) fine rice flour

75 g (2½ oz) gluten-free cornflour (cornstarch)

45 g (1½ oz) soy flour

1 teaspoon xanthan gum (optional)

55 g (2 oz) castor (superfine) sugar

160 g (5¾ oz) butter

4–5 tablespoons iced water

FILLING
550 g (1 lb 4 oz) trimmed rhubarb, cut into 3 cm (1¼ inch) pieces

½ cup sugar

¼ cup brown sugar

¾ cup castor (superfine) sugar

200 g (7 oz) reduced-fat cream cheese

⅓ cup fine rice flour

4 eggs

pure icing (confectioner's) sugar, for dusting

To make the pastry, sift the flours and xanthan gum three times into a bowl (or mix well with a whisk to ensure they are well combined). Tranfer to a food processor, add the castor sugar and butter and process until it resembles fine breadcrumbs. With the motor running, add the iced water, a tablespoon at a time, until the mixture forms a soft dough. Gently turn the pastry out onto a bench dusted with gluten-free cornflour and knead for 2–3 minutes or until smooth. Wrap in plastic film and rest in the refrigerator for 30 minutes.

Preheat the oven to 200°C (400°F). Grease a 23 cm (9 inch) flan tin. Roll out the pastry until large enough to line the tin. Ease the pastry into the tin and trim the edges. Line with baking paper and fill with baking beads or rice. Blind-bake for 10–15 minutes or until lightly browned. Remove from oven and leave to cool slightly. Reduce the oven temperature to 160°C (315°F).

To make the filling, combine the rhubarb and sugar in a large saucepan of boiling water and cook for 10 minutes or until tender. Drain. Using electric beaters, combine the rhubarb, brown sugar, castor sugar, cream cheese and rice flour in a medium bowl. Add the eggs, one at a time, beating well between additions. Pour into the pastry base and bake for 30–35 minutes or until set. Cool to room temperature, then refrigerate for 3 hours. Serve dusted with icing sugar.

◇ *This recipe is unsuitable for people with lactose intolerance unless consumed as a small serve.*

Glossary

Almond meal

Almond meal is almonds ground into a flour-like texture, and is often used in baking. It is typically the base of flourless cakes.

Amaranth

Amaranth is an ancient, high-protein grain. Amaranth flour is not generally used on its own in baking as it has a very strong taste; it works better in flour blends. Amaranth is also used to make breakfast cereal.

Arrowroot

Arrowroot is made from a tropical American plant. It is virtually tasteless and is very low in protein. It makes a gel when used as a flour to thicken, so is useful for thickening fruit sauces, but is not suitable for cheese or savoury sauces.

Baking powder

Baking powder is a raising agent. Not all baking powders are gluten-free – always check the label before buying. A simple recipe for baking powder is 1 teaspoon cream of tartar and ½ teaspoon bicarbonate of soda. This can be added to 1 cup of a gluten-free flour blend to make it 'self-raising'.

Besan flour

Besan is a roasted chickpea flour, often used in Indian cooking, and is an ideal substitute for soy flour for people who are soy intolerant. Like soy, it is high in protein and has a strong taste so is best used as a small contributor to a gluten-free flour blend. Gram flour is another type of chickpea flour.

Buckwheat

Despite its name, buckwheat is not related to wheat at all – it is actually a member of the rhubarb family. It has a strong nutty flavour and is often made into flour and used in recipes such as pancakes.

CMC (*food additive 466*)

CMC (Carboxymethylcellulose) is a water-soluble product extracted from cellulose fibre, and assists in providing food elasticity and retaining moisture in baked products. Use it in a similar way to xanthan gum.

Cornflour (cornstarch)

Gluten-free cornflour must be made from maize (corn). In some countries (including Australia and New Zealand) flour made from wheat can be called cornflour, so check the label. It has little taste, is low in protein, and makes an excellent addition to a gluten-free flour blend. It is perfect for thickening sauces.

Cornmeal

Cornmeal (also called polenta) is ground corn. It varies in grades from fine to coarse, and can be used as an alternative to breadcrumbs, but is often cooked to a porridge-like consistency or firmer to make a cornbread. It is available in supermarkets.

Guar gum (*food additive 412*)

This is a type of vegetable gum used in food manufacture and is also available for home baking. It is the ground seed of a plant called *Cyamopsis tetragonolobus*. Guar gum has a similar function to xanthan gum and CMC – it helps with food elasticity and moisture retention in baked products. It is available from health-food shops.

Millet

Not commonly used, but certainly gluten-free, millet is a grass seed that can be used to make porridge. The grains can also be cooked like rice and used as a basis for salads or savoury side dishes. Available from health-food shops.

Potato flour

Potato flour is virtually tasteless, and is made from the starch of the potato. It can be used to thicken sauces in sweet and savoury dishes, however, the sauce will become a little 'stretchy' or gel-like. It is a great addition to a gluten-free flour blend, especially when being used for cakes and muffins, and substitutes well for tapioca flour and arrowroot. It is available in Asian grocery stores.

Quinoa

Pronounced 'keen-wah', quinoa can be used in a variety of ways: as pasta and flour, and as the whole grain it can be cooked like rice and used as a basis for salads or savoury side dishes. It has a slightly bitter taste. Available from health-food shops.

Rice flour

White rice flour is the main contributor to a gluten-free flour blend and is an essential addition to any gluten-free pantry. The texture ranges from gritty to fine – fine rice flour is preferable and is readily available in Asian grocery shops. It has a neutral taste and can be used as a thickener for sauces and gravies. Brown rice flour is also available and can be used in gluten-free baking to increase the fibre content.

Soy flour

Soy flour is a high-protein flour made from soy beans. It can have a strong flavour, and is sometimes bitter. Bitterness decreases with cooking, but it is better to purchase debittered soy flour if possible. Soy flour is best used as a small, but essential part of a gluten-free flour blend. It is available from health-food shops.

Tapioca flour (cassava)

Tapioca flour is made from the dried starch of cassava root. It has little flavour, is low in protein and is a useful addition to a gluten-free flour blend. It can be used to thicken sauces in sweet and savoury dishes, however, the sauce will become a little 'stretchy' and gel-like. It is a good substitute for potato flour and arrowroot. Available in Asian grocery stores and some health-food shops.

Xanthan gum (*food additive 415*)

Xanthan gum is a vegetable gum used to assist in providing baked goods with elasticity and keeping them moist. It is a cream-coloured powder made from the ground, dried cell coat of a laboratory-grown micro-organism called *Xanthomonas campestris*. It is the most common vegetable gum used in gluten-free cooking, though guar gum or CMC can be used instead. Approximately 1–2 teaspoons are used per baking recipe. Available from health-food shops.

Acknowledgements

I am very fortunate to be surrounded by so many people who have supported me. Thanks to everyone, for making my love of food a fun and entertaining journey.

To my beautiful and very dear family – you are the most wonderful people and I am so glad you are who you are. I am sure you know the special place you have in my heart. Thanks to Marty for an amazing fifteen years.

To my friends, long and strong. Thanks for all the laughs and fun times sharing gluten-free foods – good and bad. Developing recipes should always be such fun!

A special thank you to Jodie Clifford, a selfless, beautiful friend who has offered me much support on more than one occasion. Jode – you are so brilliant.

To Rosie, Paul, Alex and Nick – a lovely family with hearts of gold.

Many thanks to all at the Coeliac Society, the Department of Gastroenterology at Box Hill Hospital, Professor Peter Gibson, Dr Bob Anderson, Dr Jason Tye-Din, Dr Ben Katz and Tobie Puttock – I feel thankful and privileged to have worked with you. Thanks also to my patients who give me such a sense of purpose.

And to the wonderful team at Penguin. No-one could ask for a more friendly group of people to work with! To my editor Rachel Carter – sincere thanks for your wonderful and tireless work. And to publisher Julie Gibbs for believing, Ingrid Ohlsson for inspiration, photographer Ian Wallace and stylist Louise Pickford for making these recipes look so appealing, home

economists Jennifer Tolhurst and Theressa Klein for deliciousness, and Megan Baker for her brilliance in design.

To the friends, colleagues and acquaintances who have not been specifically mentioned, I thank you too. The wonderful thing about life is that we are shaped by our experiences, and I thank you for helping to shape me.

Index